Making the Tough
       Leading Marines

A Practical Guide for Leaders

By Col Lance A. McDaniel, USMC (ret.)

Contents

Preface

I have been a student of leadership all my adult life. During my 30-year career as an Officer of Marines, I found that I was always learning new leadership lessons. Often, my learning was acquired experientially through encounters with people during the process of performing my normal duties, but sometimes it was a product of some intense, high-stress situation or circumstance. I really did not realize how many simple leadership lessons I acquired until I started looking back in contemplation of my career as I sought to write a speech for my retirement ceremony. Rather than give a "typical" retirement speech, I told anecdotal stories which highlighted some interesting event or period in my career. The speech was easy for me to give, because I was reliving and relating people events in a narrative style. Afterward, I received significant positive feedback from the speech, which planted a seed in my mind. Perhaps there was something useful in this drill beyond the giving of a singular speech. Maybe I could capture these anecdotal episodes in a short chapter format and associate the story with a leadership lesson.

Libraries are full of leadership and management books, with new books being published all the time. The problem is that all too many are written from an academic perspective and are dense and difficult to digest for practical application. Others are written by successful business executives or sports coaches, who only talk about their successes, and ignore their failures, with the presumption that if you model their successful behavior, you too can be a success like they were. If only it were so! I wanted to take a different approach. I wanted to share both my successes and my failures, and what I learned from both. I resolved to capture what I learned in a transparent and direct fashion, something that would be accessible for leaders in all stages of their careers; and I ultimately wanted to transcend military leadership, and present something that would be useful to leaders in both business and government.

The stories are often quite personal in nature, because I believed that to connect with me and my point, the reader must know who I am. I am unapologetically drawing from my military experiences and using military examples, but I want the reader to make the broader application of the concept I discuss. For instance, where I speak of a battalion commander, you could substitute "Director," and regimental commander could be roughly equated to "Executive Director." I believe these lessons have universal applicability, and I leave it to the reader to determine how he or she decides to use them. I have written this in a fashion whereby each chapter represents a discrete leadership lesson and can stand alone. Readers can choose to read this work straight through or take singular chapters and tackle them as individual leadership case studies. The chapters follow my career chronologically, so in some ways the reader will be able to see a progression as I matured as a leader, and the lessons tend to become a little more complex and nuanced. What follows is my attempt to share some of what I learned with the express purpose of helping others to benefit from my experiences. Some stories are serious, and some have ample humor. I hope the reader finds them engaging and useful.

Chapter One: A Lesson from Burning Powder

Managing Risk in Practical Decision-Making

I had the great pleasure of serving as an artillery officer throughout my career. The Marine Corps is organized to fight as a Marine Air Ground Task Force—an integrated organization which is centered on the infantryman on the ground. Artillery's purpose is to provide all-weather fire support to the infantry. I love the artillery because it is so mission-oriented and technically and logistically challenging. To become and remain effective, artillery units must train rigorously in field conditions, including live-fire exercises that are deliberately designed to simulate combat conditions.

After my initial training, I began my career at Camp Lejeune, North Carolina. A couple times a year my artillery regiment would "deploy" to Ft. Bragg, a few hours' drive away to conduct training exercises. During one such training exercise, I was serving as a Battery Executive Officer (XO), and one of my responsibilities was to collect and burn the unused powder increments. Artillery powder comes in a series of bags, and normally there would be several small bags of unused powder increments from every round fired—and these bags must be disposed of by incineration. After one long day of firing artillery, we had accumulated a large quantity of these powder bags. The battery was moving to a new firing position, so I gathered up a team of Marines for my powder burning detail, selected an open area, lined up my powder bags in a long line just as I had been taught. I checked the wind and verified that it was blowing gently back in my direction at the start of my line of powder. I instructed one of my Marines to light the powder (something all artillery Marines love to do for some reason). The flame immediately leaped up high as the powder began to aggressively burn—with flames perhaps 15 feet high. Unfortunately, that is when my luck changed, because the wind shifted directions, and picked up dramatically. Now the wind was blowing the flames away from me in the direction of a line of tall pine trees which populate most of the training areas at Ft Bragg. I watched in horror as a couple pine trees started smoking from the heat of the nearby flames! During those long moments, I watched my nascent career as a Marine artillery officer flicker before my eyes in the form of this intense flame. I could see myself as the young officer responsible for burning down a training range at Ft Bragg (an Army base no less). Perhaps God intervened, because the wind died down, the powder burned out, and the pine trees stopped smoking. We quickly poured water on the ashes of the burned powder as adrenaline still coursed through my veins. Wow! That was a close call, I thought. We mounted up in our tactical vehicles and I led the team to rejoin the rest of the battery—with my mind still swirling around my recent misadventure.

What did I learn from that episode? Once I had a chance to consider it, I reasoned that I had not performed a sufficiently thorough analysis of what *could* happen. I had focused exclusively on the current situation and set of circumstances and had not considered dynamic aspects of the situation. Had I taken a little more time to "worst case" my layout decisions, I could have perhaps foreseen that a significant wind shift might put the pine trees, which seemed at a safe distance under current conditions, within the reach of aggressive flames.

Lesson Learned

I believe what I learned from this powder burning incident has broader applicability for other leaders as well. Leaders confront decisions every day, some mundane and some with potentially serious consequences. When considering an important decision, I learned that it was wise to examine possible alternate outcomes beyond the one I initially anticipated, particularly if the circumstances were not as they appeared, or the circumstances changed. My experience with burning powder presented a safety hazard, but for most of the decisions that leaders make, safety is not the concern, but there are many other forms of risk that can and should be considered. Identifying and controlling risk is one of the most important functions of leadership at every level. *Before you burn your powder, make sure you recognize the implications of a change in the wind.*

Chapter Two: "Sir, we know you by your walk!"

The Importance of Leader Identity

When I was a lieutenant, my Marines had a saying, "If it ain't raining, we ain't training!" It seemed like whenever we "went to the field" for live-fire artillery training, the weather abruptly turned foul. Sometimes the weather was so bad, so wretched, that my Marines and I found a strange, dark sense of humor in our situation. We would literally find ourselves laughing at how cold, wet, and miserable we were! However, as I would later learn in combat, to be able to support the infantry, you must be prepared to operate in the most difficult circumstances. We trained all day and well into the night. In fact, nighttime training requires special attention because it can be decidedly more difficult that daytime training—so we did a great deal of our training during hours of darkness.

On one particularly dark, cold, and windy night, I was walking along the "gun line" (the row of howitzers with their associated truck, equipment, and cannon crew) as I usually did, and I came upon one of my gun crews who spoke out to me quietly as I approached in the pitch blackness. "Good evening, Sir!" I responded, "Gents, how did you know it was me?" "Sir, we know you by your walk!" I had not realized that the sound of my

Chapter Three: An Examination of Loyalty

In a perfect world, all young leaders would serve with the best leaders, people who epitomize selfless service, professional competence, emotional intelligence, and a concern for the well-being and professional development of their whole team. Unfortunately, that has not consistently been my experience. Even in the best organizations, leaders like that are not common enough, and the reality is that many people will have to work with a boss who is difficult, one who takes much of the fun out of serving the organization. What do you do when you have trouble respecting the leadership of your boss? I wish I had been better prepared to answer that question as a young officer.

When I was a lieutenant, I served my first tour at Camp Lejeune, North Carolina as a member of Battery 'C', 1st Battalion, 10th Marines. I had two different battery commanders, and although I learned from both, neither epitomized the leadership qualities that I have come to respect, and they were both difficult men with whom to serve.

After Saddam Hussein invaded Kuwait in 1990, my battalion deployed to the Persian Gulf region with Regimental Combat Team 2, as the ground component of the 4th Marine Expeditionary Brigade. I was the accountability, we promptly reported the loss to our battalion headquarters which was located aboard one of the other ships. Supply procedures required an investigation of the matter. Unfortunately, the Battalion Commander did not have any people aboard our ship other than the officers of our battery. Rather than go to the trouble to "cross-deck" an investigating officer from another ship, the Battalion Commander assigned me as the investigating officer. Clearly, I was not an ideal choice, because I would be forced to investigate my own boss, the Battery Commander. It is not the choice that I would have made under the circumstances; nevertheless, I recognized that I had a duty to perform, and I took that duty quite seriously. I interviewed and obtained statements from people involved, including the Battery Commander. I reviewed all applicable rules and regulations, particularly that part of the Supply Manual which dealt with the subject of culpability. I spoke with an expert on supply accountability, the Regimental Supply Officer. Finally, I typed up my investigation, and packaged it in a large legal envelop, along with the sworn statements I received. I gave the legal envelop to the Battalion Commander when he next visited our ship, less than a week later. It was an awkward moment. I recommended that Captain White, my Battery Commander be held culpable for the loss of the binoculars. The Battalion Commander accepted the product and thanked me, and that was the last I heard of the issue—until weeks later when my Battery Commander approached me to inform me that the Battalion Commander was "writing the binoculars off," which meant that they were being removed from the unit supply account, and that no one would be held culpable. My boss had a wry smile on his face as he told me that I had showed a lot of nerve and courage to find him culpable for the loss. I think his emotions were mixed between being personally relieved and respecting me for my principled approach to the matter.

I really do not think that the Battery Commander held the issue against me, because after we returned from the deployment, Captain White made me his battery Executive Officer. However, our relationship was no less tense. I learned the duties of the battery Executive Officer by initially modelling what I had observed from the previous executive officers with whom I had served. I had a lot to learn, and unfortunately, the Battery Commander was simply not a good teacher. Nevertheless, we had a strong team of lieutenants and staff non-commissioned officers, and we performed well, both in our frequent field training exercises and in our work in garrison. At one point, we deployed for training out to Marine Corps Air Ground Combat Training Center, Twenty-nine Palms, California to participate in a Combined Arms Exercise (CAX). The CAX is an intense command, they will often have great difficulty understanding what it is really like to be the lonesome person in charge. Ultimately, that is how I handled my relationship with my Battery Commander, Captain White. I was loyal to him, but more than that, I was loyal to the office he held. I did not agree with him much of the time, but I carried out his orders with the same energy and commitment as if I did. Subordinate leaders need to be very careful about allowing the poison of disloyalty to seep into their minds, because once there, it spreads very fast, and is very difficult to control. If you find it challenging to be loyal to the person in charge, at least fasten your loyalty to the office to which that leader has been duly and properly assigned. Remember that you can learn a great deal from those whose leadership style is quite different than your own, even if that equates to what not to do. Finally, keep in mind that "this too will pass," and you are strong enough to bear up until it does.

Chapter Four: Trust Your Own Instincts to Make the Right Decision

As a young company grade officer, I served a tour of duty at the Marine Corps Recruit Training Depot, Parris Island, South Carolina. That assignment was one of the most rewarding of my early career because I learned so much, and had the opportunity to serve with some of the finest non-commissioned officers in the Marine Corps. One of the many unique aspects of the Marine Corps is our entry-level training experience. Although it has certainly evolved over the years, one common theme is the intensity of the training experience, and the transformative effect that this intense training has on the young people who accept the challenge to become Marines. I had the chance to participate in the management of this unique training experience. Having been deployed in support of Operations DESERT SHIELD and DESERT STORM, I knew that ours was a serious business, and that we could be called up on short notice to deploy to combat. Our mission at Parris Island was to transform civilians into America's finest warriors. The men and women most directly responsible for this process were the Marine Drill Instructors. The Marine Corps selected these seasoned professionals from all occupational specialties, particularly from the combat arms like infantry and artillery. The Marine Drill

Instructor is a unique breed—because of the special emphasis on their mission and the high degree of respect conferred on those few who earn the title of Drill Instructor. The campaign cover (or "Smokey hat") which they wear quickly distinguishes them from all others.

Early in my tour at Parris Island, having been assigned as a Series Commander and completed the requisite preparatory training, I began my first training cycle with great enthusiasm and excitement. My series consisted of three training platoons, each led by a Senior Drill Instructor and two or three other drill instructors. My relationship with my three Senior Drill Instructors was not unlike a company commander with his platoon commanders.

One morning, soon after physical training, one of my Senior Drill Instructors came to my office to speak with me. I asked him what was on his mind. "Sir, one of our recruits took some pills last night." I asked, "Is he all right?" "Yes sir, he is fine. He apparently took about seven Tylenol pills." I asked, "Oh, what did the doctors say about this?" "Sir, we did not send him down to Medical because he is physically fine, and he just wants to go home." I realized that my Senior Drill Instructor was probably right about the young man's motivation, but it was a suicide gesture, nonetheless.

However, having been on the job for just over a week, I was disinclined to disagree with my Senior Drill Instructor. I just told him to send the recruit to me so that I could interview him myself. This he did, and the young recruit confirmed his intention—that he was not suicidal, he was mostly just homesick. I sent him back to his platoon to continue the training routine. Soon thereafter, I sought out the Company Commander and told him about the incident. He asked me, "What did Medical say?" "Sir, we did not send him to Medical." He asked, "Why not?" "Sir, the Senior Drill Instructor saw that the recruit was fine, that he was not suffering any ill effects from the drugs that he took." The Company Commander was generally mild-mannered and even-tempered, but on this occasion, he was quite firm with me. "Send him to Medical--now!" After we sent the recruit down to Medical for evaluation, I called down to speak with the doctor who examined him, and I apologized for our failure to send the recruit down to Medical as soon as we learned of his actions. In recruit training, suicide ideations and gestures, even those that do not appear genuine, are taken very seriously. I knew instinctively when I learned of the incident that the right thing to do was send the recruit down to Medical for evaluation, but I hesitated. I allowed my Senior Drill Instructor to convince me, at least temporarily, that my instinct was off base.

Chapter Five: "Gentlemen, Never Accept the Unacceptable Answer!"

Tracking Down Solutions to Problems with Determination

No young officer seeks out a staff job; that is just not why they joined the military. However, the reality for every officer in every branch of service is that over the course of their careers, they will serve repeatedly on staffs at different levels. Staff officers are often forced, in the conduct of their duties, to interface with internal and external bureaucracies. To be effective representatives of their organizations, they must pursue answers to organizational problems with dogged determination.

As a young captain, I was serving on a battalion staff as the Logistics Officer. All my fellow staff officers were likewise young and only moderately experienced. During a weekly staff meeting, our Battalion Commander, an experienced leader with an intense personality, asked the Operations Officer a question. The Operations Officer answered the question, but not satisfactorily. When the Battalion Commander probed with a follow-on question, the Operations Officer, who was a friend of mine, answered to the effect that the answer he provided, though admittedly unsatisfactory, was the answer he himself had been given by an external bureau with whom he was interfacing. The Battalion Commander gave my friend one of his "I could kill you with my eyes" looks. We soon learned that we were all going to be subjected to a "teachable moment." The Battalion Commander then replied, while staring at each of us, "Gentlemen, never accept the unacceptable answer!" We looked at each other quizzically, until finally someone gained the courage to ask the Boss the obvious question. "Sir, what is the unacceptable answer?" Without hesitation, the Battalion Commander thundered, "The answer you don't want to hear. The one you know to be wrong. Gentlemen, keep asking the question until you find someone who can give you an acceptable answer!"

Since that time, and throughout my career, I have confirmed the wisdom of my Battalion Commander's simple dictum. The point was this, when pursuing the answer to an important question I found that I could not merely accept the first answer I received, particularly if it did not align with what I believed to be correct. If the issue mattered enough for me to be personally involved, I needed to have the professional determination to tactfully press forward until I was sufficiently satisfied that I had obtained the best answer. I might be required to provide that answer to senior leaders, and I knew that to maintain my professional reputation, when I provided information, my senior leaders could rely on that information; that I had performed "due diligence" in obtaining answers.

Lesson Learned

Bureaucracies are composed of people, and unfortunately, not all people are equally motivated to help you solve your problem or provide sensible answers to your questions. Sometimes, if you are not receiving what you deem to be acceptable answers, you may be required to "elevate the issue" to someone who can provide a more satisfactory and acceptable answer to your question. Leaders have a responsibility to their organization to make decisions based on the best information they can reasonably obtain. Unfortunately, that may require the exercise of some patient, but determined inquiry. *Never accept the unacceptable answer!*

Chapter Six: Encouraging Integrity

As a young company grade officer, I served for a time as a Series Commander at Marine Corps Recruit Training Depot, Parris Island, South Carolina. For me, it was the right assignment at the right time in my career, because I think in many ways, it prepared me for the challenges ahead. A recruit training series is composed of three or four training platoons. The Series Commander is the first officer in the "chain of command," and is responsible for supervising the training process, including the adherence to all appropriate rules and regulations. The individual training platoons are led by a Senior Drill Instructor and his drill instructor team. There are normally two series per training company, and the company goes through a 12-week training cycle together.

Drill instructors are the leaders most responsible for the actual training of the recruits. They have the huge responsibility of transforming young Americans into Marines. Although all Marines are special, the drill instructors are a select group of seasoned non-commissioned officers, top performers who have proved themselves in their respective communities before they even step foot at Drill Instructor School. There they have to demonstrate that they have what it takes to teach Marine recruits, if they expect to earn the title of Marine Drill Instructor. I noticed the high level of competition that takes place between platoons during all training events, especially the graded ones. Drill instructors are naturally competitive, and what I observed was that we were subtly encouraging them to be even more competitive. Every aspect of training is carefully monitored and assessed. The training companies keep track of all the statistics; everything from injury rates to rifle range scores and physical fitness tests. Senior Drill Instructors are evaluated by their statistics, the most important being their platoon retention rate, which is the percentage of cohort recruits that they retain through the entire training cycle.

In my first training cycle, one of the platoons in my series was "winning" nearly every testable event. As the training cycle progressed, I wondered how this platoon was able to perform better than other platoons. They were "dropping" fewer recruits from training. Their first phase physical fitness test scores were higher. At the rifle range, they had fewer recruits (none) fail to at least qualify on the range (by shooting the minimum passing score), and they had the highest number of recruits earn their Expert Marksmanship badge. At the end of the training cycle, they had the highest Final Physical Fitness score by platoon average. I became a believer in the leadership abilities of the Senior Drill Instructor who managed to "win" so often. Clearly, Senior Drill Instructor "Winner" was a more effective leader than his peers--or was he?

Our company First Sergeant, a veteran of the "drill field" was now on his third tour at Parris Island. For some reason, he was less impressed with this apparently successful platoon, and I wondered why. Later, as the First Sergeant and I began to look closer at the platoon's performance, we saw evidence of what we called, "heavy-barrelling," which was jargon for drill instructors tampering with the process to improve the results in their favor. For instance, Senior Drill Instructors were required to make entries in each recruit's training record book to document counselling. I noticed that Senior Drill Instructor Winner used erasable ink for his entries, and on at least one occasion, I saw evidence that he had probably adjusted a recruit's record by cutting out an unfavorable section or simply erasing what he had previously written. Before a recruit could be dropped from training for a failure to adapt, the record had to show that the recruit had been appropriately counselled and given a chance to improve. Apparently, Senior Drill Instructor Winner made adverse comments in the books of many recruits, and then simply removed that part of the record if required. I noticed this when he nominated one of his recruits to be the Series Honor Man, the top performing recruit in the Series. The record for the recruit he nominated had obviously been recently altered. On qualification day at the Rifle Range, I had heard rumors of Senior Drill Instructor Winner's platoon using the "5.56mm pencil." (This jargon referred to the implied use of a pencil to poke a hole in the black bullseye of the target if the round did not pierce the paper there.) Obviously, that would have been cheating. At the time, I was not inclined to listen to the rumors. I was just happy that this platoon was performing so well, and since they seemed to be showing a track record of success, I saw this as more evidence of the same.

Later, based on a proven performance record, Senior Drill Instructor Winner was nominated for a meritorious promotion. Unfortunately, before he was promoted, he exposed his lack of integrity more clearly. The Battalion Sergeant Major caught him in a lie. At that point, I recalled all the times when there was evidence of "heavy barreling," and although I could not prove it, my confidence in the veracity of Winner's statistics was completely undermined.

Lesson Learned

This is not simply a story about a Senior Drill Instructor who probably cheated the system to advance his own career. Rather, I relate this story as an example of unhealthy competitiveness that we as leaders supported and fostered. As we focused on specific statistics, we showed what we prioritized, and we unknowingly incentivized our Senior Drill Instructors to focus their efforts on achieving success in those specific areas, rather than on ensuring a quality training process. This tendency to incentivize specific success metrics is not unique to recruit training, and if leaders in any organization are not careful, they can inadvertently encourage a breach of integrity in which results are achieved by undesirable means, or as it more often the case, metrics are manipulated to reflect the more positive message. We as leaders must demand and reward integrity, in both action and intention—and we should avoid creating a circumstance in which those with weak integrity are easily influenced to cheat the system that we developed. As my Grandfather used to say, *"Lock your car door and keep an honest man honest."*

Chapter Seven: "Sir, I take full responsibility"

The Power of a Timely Apology

In the mid-90's, while I was a captain stationed at Marine Corps Recruit Depot, Parris Island, South Carolina, I was assigned as the Recruit Training Regiment (RTR) Scheduling Officer, a position within the Regimental Operations Section. The Scheduling Team is responsible for creating and managing the training schedules for all 14 training companies. At times it is like a factory production line, where a change in one area can affect several other areas. The art is keeping all 14 companies on track and avoiding a "collision" with another training company. If one company arrives late for a meal or for an event, it can lead to a "snowball effect" on other companies. Most of the time, we were able to manage the schedule well enough that there were no problems. However, occasionally, we made a mistake.

One morning, I received a phone call from a friend of mine who was the Operations Officer for one of the Training Battalions. He informed me of a scheduling problem involving one of their training companies. I told him that we would work to resolve the problem. Frankly, I was surprised that the problem had not been brought to our attention before that time. The mistake was ours, but neither the Training Company nor the Training Battalion had noticed the problem, until that time—and it was going to be hard to avoid an impact on training at that late stage. I hung up with him after telling him we would do what we could to straighten it out. A very short time later, my phone rang again, and it was my friend again. This time, I could hear the concern in his voice. He told me that his boss, the Battalion Commander, had learned of the scheduling problem (presumably from speaking with the Training Company Commander), and he was hot. In fact, he was on his way up to the Regimental Headquarters right then to speak with the Regimental Commander on this issue. I thanked my friend for the warning and hung up the phone. Now what?

I decided to address the Battalion Commander myself on the issue. Soon he appeared in the hallway, and I said, "Sir, I understand that there has been a scheduling mix-up with one of your Training Companies. I take full responsibility for this mistake, and I want to apologize. We are working now to resolve the issue in the best way we can." As soon as I addressed him, he stopped to look at me, and I could tell he was angry. However, when he heard me apologize and assume full responsibility, his whole demeanor changed. He paused before he spoke, and I sensed that he was taken aback by my apology, something he had not expected. Finally, he told me that, "Actually, I think that we too bear some of the responsibility for this mix-up, because we should have caught it earlier, and brought it to your attention." I responded, "Sir, that would have been helpful, but it is our responsibility to create and manage these training schedules, and on this occasion, we made an error. I'm sorry for the trouble this has caused." The Battalion Commander thanked me for that, and realized he really had no reason to bring the matter up with the Regimental Commander, given that he realized it was an honest mistake that we were working to rectify, that we apologized for the mistake, and that regardless of my attempt to "own the mistake," his team really should have caught it earlier. He turned and departed the Regimental Headquarters building, albeit at a much slower pace. Afterward, I reflected on the interchange. At one brief moment in the conversation, I had the strange feeling that we were playing tug-o-war with responsibility for the scheduling mistake—and maybe that was not a bad thing.

Lesson Learned

Long before this episode, I understood the importance of taking responsibility for the performance of the team, and "owning it" when something went wrong. People respect a leader who can acknowledge a mistake and accept responsibility. It is usually easier to get on with the effort to resolve a problem if the leaders involved acknowledge the mistake. I learned a lesson from this episode on the power of a well-timed and genuine apology. I showed the Battalion Commander that we understood the impact of our error, and that once we learned of it, were working to resolve it. The Battalion Commander was angry when he arrived at the headquarters building, but my apology helped him calm down and see the issue more clearly. People make mistakes in human interactions, and a prompt and meaningful apology, one that shows you understand the impact of your error on the other person and their team, is more than appropriate. This kind of apology can actually be powerful. I think there are three elements to it: it must be timely, it must be genuine, and it must demonstrate that you are looking at the issue from the other person's vantage point, and understand the effect that your mistake had on the other person. In some circumstances, your apology can lead to a stronger relationship than what existed before the incident, because you can earn respect for being responsible and sensitive to the needs of others. *When your team makes a mistake that adversely affects another team, be ready to "own it," and apologize.*

Chapter Eight: Leadership at the Point of Friction

When I was a battery commander, I had a Battery Gunnery Sergeant (E7) named Gunnery Sergeant Martinez who proved to be exactly the right man for the job. The "Battery Gunny" as he is known works with the Battery Executive Officer to run the battery. He takes part in operational planning and oversees all the unit logistics requirements. Gunnery Sergeant Martinez was old for his rank. He knew he was not competitive for promotion, but he was one of the most reliable, solid leaders with whom I have served, a real professional that I found I could always count upon to "make things happen."

One of the things that Gunnery Sergeant Martinez was particularly good at doing was anticipating the "point of friction" in an operation and locating himself there in advance so that he could oversee the process and help the unit to push through the friction. The point of friction is a phase of an event that represents added complexity or lack of surety on the part of participants. Often it is something that the organization has little or no experience at performing or has not performed recently. The point of friction may present a "bottleneck" in the flow of an operation or event, and it often occurs when two or more systems are interacting. Though the point of friction is usually not the main effort, it may undermine the accomplishment of the main effort if it is not properly supervised. Gunnery Sergeant Martinez was an experienced artilleryman, and I believe it was a combination of his experience and his uncanny level of common sense and operational savvy that made him so effective at anticipating the point of friction. It could be something simple enough; but whether it was a critical turn in the road during a long night convoy movement, or a link up with a logistics unit to take on fuel, Gunnery Sergeant Martinez was always there, overseeing and orchestrating the event.

I learned an important lesson from Gunnery Sergeant Martinez, that as a leader, I needed to anticipate the points of friction and ensure that I was prepared to address them. From that period forward and throughout my career, I made a concerted effort to anticipate the point of friction in an event and put plans in place to mitigate risk. I knew I could not personally be physically present at all points of friction, but I could ensure that a leader I trusted was there and could supervise the activity by providing on-site direction.

Late in my career I served on the Joint Staff as an

Assistant Deputy Director in the Strategic Plans and Policy Directorate. The United States was going to launch some cruise missiles into Syria during hours of darkness. We anticipated a late-night Press Conference at the Pentagon to discuss the strike. Given that this was to be a Coalition operation, we wanted to bring representatives of key Allied Nations in to the press room at the Pentagon to stand with our leaders as they discussed the operation with members of the press. In this case, the point of friction was the act of linking up with two representatives from two of our Allies and escorting them to a staging room away from the eager press immediately prior to the Press Conference. I selected one of our officers earlier in the day for this duty, and then went with him as we made connections with all the people who would play a role in orchestrating this Press Conference. I even walked the terminal end of the route that I wanted him to take with the two Allies. I wanted to leave nothing to chance, so I personally ensured that our man knew his role and what we expected of him. Although I was quite busy at the time, I knew this had to go smoothly, and it was sufficiently complicated that it required my attention. In the end, there were some complications, but we managed to overcome those, and we had our two Allies in position for the late-night Press Conference.

Lesson Learned

Sometimes it requires the wisdom that is derived from experience to be able to anticipate an activity's point of friction. What I learned was that leaders need to be thinking about possible points of friction as they make their plans. The point of friction does not have to be an obviously important aspect of an event or activity. Sometimes, something as seemingly mundane as escorting a couple senior executives to the right place for a top-level meeting, will represent the point of friction. However, the point of friction is more often the intersection of two independent systems or organizations whose interaction must occur smoothly for the event or operation to progress on schedule. I learned that I needed to direct the attention of one of the leaders on my team to this point of friction, so that he or she could supervise it as required. *Learn to anticipate your point of friction.*

Chapter Nine: "Take the Message to Garcia."

As a senior captain I had the pleasure of serving on the 15th Marine Expeditionary Unit (MEU), which is based out of Camp Pendleton, California. The MEUs deploy as a team with a Navy Amphibious Ready Group on three amphibious ships, and their mission is to support Combatant Commanders out in their respective Theaters of Operation around the world. We were scheduled to deploy to the Western Pacific and then proceed to the Middle East. I was the 15th MEU Fire Support Officer, which meant that I was responsible for coordinating all fire support: air, ground, and sea-based, for the MEU.

One day my boss, the MEU Operations Officer, Lieutenant Colonel Rob Barrow, called me into his office. "Mac (my nickname), you've got WESTPAC (western Pacific) training. Do you have any questions?" I asked if he had any further instructions. "No. Take the message to Garcia." When I was a cadet at Texas A&M University, my Senior Marine Officer Instructor, Major John D. McGuire, had instructed us to read the short book, *Take the Message to Garcia*" by Elbert Hubbard, a book that has also been on the Commandant's Reading List for years. The point of the book is that, when your boss gives you a mission, and only general instructions, it is your responsibility to use your native intelligence and resourcefulness to carry out the assignment without the benefit or constraint of being told *how* to accomplish the task. When my boss told me to "take the message to Garcia," he was essentially telling me that I was empowered to accomplish this mission in the best way I saw fit, and that he had every confidence that I did not require detailed instructions in order to achieve success. Normally, I liked getting broad guidance like this because it afforded me great independence of action. My problem at that very moment was that I did not even know what countries in the western Pacific we would be visiting during our deployment, let alone the opportunities that might be available to hone our skills. Ultimately, we put together a multi-day training package for the entire MEU in Singapore. As we were under way, steaming for the western Pacific, we stopped briefly in Hong Kong, and I picked a small team of planners and flew from Hong Kong to Singapore to finalize the planning and prepare for the reception of the MEU. The result was a challenging and rewarding training exercise with the Singaporean military. The whole affair was quite the success. My reward? "Mac, that was a good exercise. Now you have responsibility for training in

Kuwait. Any questions?"

As a young leader, sometimes it feels empowering and exciting to be challenged with broad, general directions. It forces you to use all your mental faculties—to stretch a bit (or a lot). I have also learned in my career that some people operate well with inexplicit instructions, what we in the Marine Corps refer to as "Commander's Intent." Others find that non-specific approach to be highly stressful, and with them I knew I needed to provide more detailed guidance, both up front and throughout the project's duration. Neither approach is wrong. The art is learning what works best with your people in any given circumstance. To do that, you really need to get to know your people, to understand their individual strengths and weakness, and determine what motivates them.

Lesson Learned

When I was given an opportunity as a planner to operate with a wide range of independence, I learned something about myself. I learned that I was resourceful and that I derived no small amount of satisfaction from envisioning a project and applying myself to bring it to a successful conclusion. I learned that I did not need, nor even desire, to have someone like my boss, explain to me what I needed to accomplish. I could determine all of that myself. I would need help, but it was up to me to determine what resources I would require for a given project. *Take the Message to Garcia!*

Chapter Ten: Tact in Inter-personal Relations

Some people learn vicariously, and others have to experience something in order to really internalize the learning points. Although I would like to say that I was a vicarious learner, the reality is that I was more of the latter. As a young officer, I mistakenly believed that what mattered was mission accomplishment--exclusively. I was brash and thought I knew what was best. I enjoyed working with other high-energy people, but when I encountered others who were less driven than I was, I tended to impose my will on them, usually without even realizing that I was doing so. One day, my boss, Lieutenant Colonel Rob Barrow, who was quite a bit older and more experienced than I was, pulled me aside and said, "Mac, you are like a bull in a china shop!" I just grinned at him. At the time, I thought he was giving me a compliment! Later, as I reflected on the inter-change, I realized that my boss did not intend to compliment me, but rather to teach me. I began to consider what he said and why he would have said it to me; after all, I had a strong track record of succeeding at every assignment. So what was the problem?

Many people mistakenly believe that in the military, being as hierarchal as it is, leaders direct and followers receive and comply with direction. The reality is that the military, being composed of people like all organizations are, is much more participatory in task assignment and execution. People work in teams and team dynamics are always in play. People tend to work best in an environment in which they know they are valued for their contributions. I have found that the best and most effective leaders are those who not only accomplish the mission, but also display high emotional intelligence as well. In team dynamics, a person will often be working with others who are of similar seniority within the organization, and leadership may take the form of advocacy for a particular course of action or initiative. Many people tend to work best in a more collegial atmosphere, even in difficult or stressful circumstances. No one enjoys working with someone who is insensitive to their opinions and preferences, even if that person is decidedly senior to them. When Lieutenant Colonel Barrow conveyed his observation of me, I came to the realization that I was not always the kind of person with whom others would enjoy serving, because I often lacked tact and, though I was generally polite and courteous enough, I could be rather insensitive to other positions and perspectives. I could plow over others with weaker wills without even realizing that I was doing so. In short, I still had a great deal of learning to do in the area of inter-personal relations. From that point forward, I made a deliberate effort to improve my emotional intelligence, to sensitize myself to others' perspectives. In some cases, this required that I slow down and spend more time actively listening, and less time planning and directing. For me as a young officer, this was a subtler, less obvious lesson, but as I matured as a leader, I came to understand that this was every bit as important to my success and the team's morale as my singular drive for mission accomplishment.

Over the course of my career, I had the great pleasure of serving with some fine officers, and I actively sought to learn as much as I could from all of them, even those who had distinctly different personalities and leadership styles than my own. I wanted to learn from both their strengths and their shortcomings. Oddly enough, even in an organization as elite as the Marine Corps, I found that there are only a few leaders who are truly extraordinary. One of the leaders who fit this description in my estimation was Lieutenant General Richard C. Zilmer, USMC (ret.), with whom I served when he commanded the 15th MEU as a colonel. Colonel Zilmer was the one leader I sought most to emulate as I matured as a leader myself. He had an incredible ability to obtain best efforts from his whole team, perhaps in part because every one of us loved him and wanted to always give our utmost in support of his agenda. He was able to expose his humanity without in any way seeming weak—in fact, it seemed like it made him appear stronger. He was a coach kind of leader, one whose energetic and gregarious personality proved infectious to all those with whom he came in contact. He was loyal to his team, and we all felt that loyalty to him as well. One measure of a good leader is whether his people are better after having served with him; and that was absolutely true with Colonel Zilmer. Colonel Zilmer had extremely high emotional intelligence, and that is a quality that I sought to improve upon myself. This process of change did not occur instantly; however, over time, I sought to be more the kind of leader for which I myself preferred to work, one with who people enjoyed serving, even though the expectations of performance remained quite high.

Lesson Learned

Sometimes even top performing people need for someone to pull them aside and provide some coaching and mentoring. In my case, I needed a dose of honesty at that point in my career so that I could improve in the way I dealt with both my team and others outside my team. Without that, I would probably not have been as effective in interpersonal relations as I gained in seniority and led larger and more complex organizations. I matured as a leader in part because I had a boss who, during a teachable moment, told me I was like a bull in a china shop; and I was sufficiently introspective to absorb that lesson, and I was sufficiently committed to improvement to work diligently over time to be a better team-mate to everyone. *I knew I wanted to be a Zilmer kind of leader.*

Chapter Eleven: "Let's Make That Decision Together"

Taking Care of Your People

Leaving your family and heading off on a deployment is difficult. For me, it really never became easier with my subsequent deployments. I joined the Marine Corps knowing that I was signing up for many long deployments, and I always felt good about our mission when one of my units deployed. However, saying good-bye to my wife and children was just tough. I used to get a bit of a sick feeling in my stomach, and I lost all my appetite right before a deployment, not because I did not want to go, but there is this strange feeling of putting away my role of husband and father as I focused on my mission ahead. When my Dad returned from Vietnam, I was two years old, and I did not recognize him. I regarded him as a stranger. I know that being away for over a year was tough for him, and the fact that his little boy did not even recognize him when he first returned made it even difficult. All of my deployments were difficult for the same reason.

As a captain I deployed with the 15th Marine Expeditionary Unit (MEU) for a six-month period. I left behind my wife, Rhonda, and our two daughters,

Rebekah (7) and Elizabeth (4) at the time. We had endured a six-month work-up period, so we were ready to go. Also, I knew that my wife was resourceful and quite capable of handling things in my absence; after all, she was a Marine wife!

Our deployment was going well, and we were extremely busy. We conducted training in Hawaii, Singapore, and Kuwait. As I had been the principal architect of the planning for training in both Singapore and Kuwait, I was feeling the satisfaction that comes with plans coming to successful fruition. Then all that satisfaction came to a screeching halt. I was ashore in Kuwait, performing some advance planning in order to receive the MEU once they arrived. The MEU Commander, Colonel Rich Zilmer, called me from the command ship. He had received some very bad news from the home front. He informed me that one of my daughters, Elizabeth, was very sick, and that I needed to call home immediately. This was the late 1990's, so calling home from the Middle East was not quite as easy as it is today. However, I was able to get through to Rhonda, and she informed me that my four-year old had a three-inch tumor in her abdomen, and was due to go into surgery in two days to have it removed. I am sure that she was quite clear with me that it was cancerous, but I could not absorb that information. I told her that I would call back in a couple days to see if it was benign or not. After the call, I spoke with Colonel Zilmer again. He wanted to discuss sending me home, but I was too absorbed in the work that I had been doing, and I told him about the surgery, and that the tumor would be categorized once it had been removed. I was not sure I had convinced him to allow me to stay. He concluded the conversation by telling me, "We'll make that decision together." I went about my business the next morning, but I had a huge sense of something ominous that I was unable to block out of my mind, and it started to eat at me. I felt like I was being torn in two pieces; one that saw my responsibility to my unit, and one that saw my responsibility to my family, specifically to my sick little girl. Later that day, unbeknownst to me, Colonel Zilmer contacted Major "Wheels" Weidley, our Air Officer, who was ashore with me doing the final planning. He told Major Weidley, "I'm sending Lance home. Please make the arrangements for his flight home to San Diego." When Major Weidley told me the news, I felt a strange emotion. Rather than feeling like I had let my unit down, I felt a sense of relief that someone made this tough decision to send me home, a decision that I simply was unable to make. The trip home was a long one, and I had too much time to think and worry. By the time I arrived to Naval Hospital, Balboa, I was mentally numb. Elizabeth was still in surgery, but I was able to sit with Rhonda as we waited. After the surgery, the doctor came out and spoke to us briefly, and he said we would know more information in the morning. A family friend drove me home to my house at Camp Pendleton. When I arrived at my house that night, it all came rushing at me, and I was literally nauseous. From that point forward, we dealt with my daughter's cancer treatment as a family. I learned that Elizabeth had Stage IV neuroblastoma, and that her prognosis was about as bleak as possible. She fought the cancer for almost two years before she succumbed to the disease, two weeks before her sixth birthday.

Lesson Learned

I will always be grateful to Colonel Zilmer for making the decision to send me home. He was able to see what I could not, that my place was back with my family. Moreover, he probably knew that despite my protestations to remain, soon enough I would be ineffective there on deployment, utterly incapable of concentrating on the job at hand. Years later when I was the Executive Officer of 3d Battalion, 11th Marines, we had a similar case with one of our captains while in the heat of combat operations in Iraq. The Battalion Commander and I agreed that the right thing to do was to send him home, and we did. It is never an easy decision to remove a key leader from a position by sending them home, knowing full well that they are not going to be returning to the unit. However, it is usually the right decision when a member of their family is seriously ill. Colonel Zilmer taught me many things, but one of the most profound was the importance of taking care of your people through genuine concern for their welfare. Although business leaders may not be faced with decisions as bleak as the decision I have described, the lesson has universal applicability. *People will follow you anywhere when they see that you genuinely care for them.*

Chapter Twelve: "Sir, I Do the Rest!"

Providing Effective Support to Others

When most young people seek out commissioned service in the Marine Corps, they have a vision of being in charge, of being placed in command of something. They see the image of a leader and think platoon commander and company or battery commander. All young officers want to be afforded the opportunity to command. The good news is that for those who make the military a career, most will have that opportunity. The other reality is that most of an officer's career is spent in positions when he or she is not in command, but rather, is serving on a staff somewhere, operating in an independent assignment, or has responsibility for a project or initiative.

I learned during my career that there are many kinds of leadership. Sometimes I was the person who shouldered the responsibility of command. On those occasions, the leadership of an organization of people was rather straightforward. On other occasions, my responsibility was more of a programmatic nature, and rather than directly leading people, I was charged with exploring future technological requirements or writing concepts that described the Marine Corps' future force.

In those latter assignments I was leading by virtue of proponency or advocacy.

I have been an Executive Officer or Deputy even more often than I commanded myself. I believe I was an effective commander at every level I commanded. However, it is quite possible that I was a more effective Executive Officer. As a captain, I had the pleasure of serving with a truly effective battalion Executive Officer, Major Steve Hogg. Major Hogg seldom raised his voice or lost his temper. He provided sage advice and counsel to the battery commanders (myself included), and he coached the battalion staff to successfully carry out the Battalion Commander's direction and intent. Major Hogg was solid and unflappable, even in stressful situations. Major Hogg was not in command, but by his actions, he provided the best support for which a commander could hope or dream. I learned a great deal about leadership from Major Hogg.

Many years later, before I became a battalion commander myself, I attended a Commanders' Course that was required of all incoming commanders. One of the speakers was then Brigadier General "Fighting Joe" Dunford, who later became the Chairman of the Joint Chiefs of Staff. I had known Brigadier General Dunford since he was a colonel, and I respected him immensely. I took detailed notes, and everything he said seemed to resonate with me. He made reference to his own experience in battalion command when he noted that he determined early in his tenure of command that wherever he was as the commander, physically or figuratively, created space where he was absent. This meant that he had to choose as deliberately where he would be absent as he did where he would be present. It also meant that he needed help spreading out his command influence to those areas in which he himself could not be present. He went on to describe his vision of a "command team" composed of his executive officer, his sergeant major (the senior enlisted advisor to the commander) and himself. He used his executive officer and his sergeant major to spread the influence of his leadership throughout the battalion. I thought that was brilliant, and that is how I sought to use my command team.

However, years before I became a commander, I served as a battalion executive officer myself. I remembered what I had learned from Major Hogg, and I made every effort to support my commander and to spread his influence to areas he could not be present. I was the Executive Officer of 3rd Battalion, 11th Marines when the 1st Marine Division deployed to Kuwait before eventually attacking into Iraq. The first phase of the assault into Iraq was labeled OPENING GAMBIT, and it only lasted a few exhausting days. The next phase of the operation called for a lightning march to Baghdad. During a short pause before we began this next phase, the Battalion Commander, Lieutenant Colonel Kirk Hymes, turned to me and said, "XO, what do you see as your role at this stage?" I imagine he expected me to answer specifically, but I replied generally. "Sir, I do the rest!" He thought for a moment and then his eyes lit up and he said, "Exactly! I will position myself with the lead element of the battalion convoy, and you take the rear." And that is how we orchestrated command of a unit that was extremely spread out chasing a fast-moving maneuver element. I was literally the last vehicle of my battalion's long convoy. For significant periods of time, we were well outside the range of our tactical radio communications with the rest of the battalion. The march to Baghdad was indescribably exhausting. Our drivers would fall asleep at the wheel if they stopped rolling, even for mere seconds. I literally had to run up and down the length of the rear convoy to bang on doors and wake drivers up so that we could keep the convoy moving—together—through enemy territory in the dark of night. During that time, it was almost as if the battalion was two separate units, because we were so far apart. Eventually, we were able to catch up and consolidate the battalion, which simplified control, but even then, I continued to focus on support functions so that the Battalion Commander could keep his attention on the unit's main effort.

Lesson Learned

I learned that for our "command team" I was able to extend the commander's influence by focusing my attention and energies in areas that were important to the commander, but outside the main effort. In that way, the commander could keep his focus on the unit's primary mission, while having confidence that all the other necessary functions were being supervised by someone who knew exactly what he wanted, and would exercise the same level of diligence and attention to detail as he would. Although this concept applies well in ground combat units in the military, it also works in other kinds of organizations, both in the public and private sector. The senior executive realizes that he or she can only focus their attention in a finite area or direction, and they will rely on others to extend their influence to important, but perhaps less critical areas. This "behind-the-scenes" orchestration and staff supervision may not garner the same level of recognition or acknowledgement, but it is the best way to help the executive succeed, and thereby ensure ongoing mission success. *Commit to provide your executive with the most effective level of support by "doing the rest!"*

Chapter Thirteen: Missing Tool Kit No. Five
Teaching a Young Leader to Do a Job Right

In the military, when something goes wrong, there is nearly always a requirement to determine what went wrong, and in many cases to determine responsibility or culpability. This requirement exists for everything from accidents that lead to serious personal injury to lost or damaged equipment. Investigations are ordered by commanders at the battalion level or above. When I was a lieutenant in an artillery battery, I was given my first command investigation. I was admonished that I should do a good job, because the Battalion Commander would be personally reviewing my work, and this might be one of the first opportunities for me to make a positive impression with him. I do not remember the topic of the investigation, or what my findings were, but I do remember the point about making a good impression with the boss for a job well done.

Fast forward many years, and I was serving as the Executive Officer of 3d Battalion, 11th Marines, an artillery battalion based at Twenty-nine Palms, California. My Battalion Supply Officer came to me to report that we were missing a Mechanic's Tool Kit, and given the dollar value, we were required to conduct an investigation into the loss. Investigations of this nature were normally assigned to lieutenants in the battalion; "another chance to excel." Accordingly, we assigned this investigation to Second Lieutenant Jones, a member of Battery 'I.' I brought the young officer into my office and gave him his instructions. Lieutenant Jones was a highly motivated young man, but I could tell that this was not what he envisioned when he considered commissioned service. Investigations of this kind are usually afforded a time constraint of several days, and Lieutenant Jones used all the time he had been allotted. The product he turned in to me was not very good. In fact, it was embarrassingly bad. I pulled out my red pen and "bled all over" the paper; then I called Lieutenant Jones in and handed the product back to him with instructions to make corrections and return it. In most cases, that would have been enough for the investigating officer to internalize the message that they needed to make the prescribed edits and improve the quality of their work. Unfortunately, that is not how this story played out. The second attempt was only marginally better than the first—so we repeated the process. The third attempt showed some improvement but was far from satisfactory. By the time of the fourth attempt, I gave up concern about processing a timely investigation, and decided that Lieutenant Jones had an important lesson to learn here, and that was much more important than the timeliness of the investigation's conclusion. On the fifth attempt, I brought in Lieutenant Jones' Battery Commander and asked that he sit down with his lieutenant and assist him in drafting a satisfactory investigative report, one that would be fit for the Battalion Commander to endorse. This time, when Lieutenant Jones turned in his product, it was satisfactory. I drafted an endorsement and the Battalion Commander signed it.

I had all but forgotten about the incident until almost 15 years later when now Lieutenant Colonel Jones met me at a ceremony. I had not seen him in years but had been monitoring his successful career from a distance. In a private moment, Lieutenant Colonel Jones told me, "Sir, I have never forgotten the lesson you taught me with tool kit number five." From his serious tone, I could tell that he understood that this lesson extended well beyond a singular investigation, and at some point, he figured that out and internalized the lesson. What was the lesson? Simply this, always do your absolute best on every project you are tasked to complete, even those you might find boring or distasteful. Earn a reputation for excellence in all things, not just the jobs you like or think you are most qualified to perform.

Lesson Learned

I do not relate this story to explain what Lieutenant

Jones learned, but rather to make the point that leaders have a responsibility to teach their new people what is expected of them, and to demand that they deliver products of high quality. Even in simple matters, leaders should not allow a substandard product to advance because the new person will not learn that they did not rise to expectations. For the new team member to learn, they may be required to stretch, and *it is your duty as a leader to help them see the way forward and hold them to the standard.*

Chapter Fourteen: "I Will Tell Him."

The Leadership Responsibility of Difficult Conversations

In 2004, my artillery battalion, 3d Battalion, 11th Marines, was ordered back to Iraq for our second combat tour. I was still the Executive Officer, but we had a new battalion commander, Lieutenant Colonel Tom Connally. Our previous combat tour had been in the role of conventional artillery, but now we were re-missioned as Task Force Military Police. Although we were based out of Camp Ramadi, we operated throughout the restive Al Anbar Province of western Iraq. While there had been a short period of relative calm immediately after our seizure of Baghdad the previous year, an insurgency was well on the rise by the time we returned to Iraq, and the Al Anbar Province was the center of the Sunni insurrection. No convoy could move anywhere on any of the roads without being at risk of attack, either by small arms, improvised explosive devices, or a more complex ambush. Our unit's principal mission was to escort logistics elements between the various forward operating bases, to ensure that they arrived with the best safety we could provide in transit. We were busy!

Camp Ramadi lies on the outskirts of the city of Ramadi, the capital of Al Anbar Province. Ramadi had become an active hub of an urban insurgency. During our tour, 2d Battalion, 4th Marines, the "Magnificent Bastards," an infantry battalion from our division, occupied key positions throughout the city itself, and conducted security patrols, day and night. It seemed like the insurgency was picking up energy, as if Ramadi lured insurgent fighters from all over the country—and beyond.

One day, I was out with one of our platoons that was providing security for a Civil Affairs Team that was meeting with Iraqi Government officials at the Government Center in Ramadi. The platoon I was with occupied a position in what was colloquially named, "RPG Alley," and there were holes in the wall behind us to attest to us how the alley acquired its name. It was broad daylight, and we all had a sense of unease about our position, feeling exposed and vulnerable. Then something happened. We looked around and all the windows and doors were shut in the buildings around us. All the store fronts had closed. Suddenly, there were no women or children anywhere! What was going on?! The tension in the air was palpable, and we felt on edge. Something felt dreadfully wrong. The platoon commander decided to position some Marines on a nearby rooftop to provide a better vantage point. We looked down the alley, and several hundred yards away, a group of men had appeared, and they seemed to be focused on us. We could not see any weapons though, so there was little we could do but wait to see how this would develop. Without thinking, I patted my full magazine pouches, and thumbed the safety on my rifle, "on" and "off." We were all in condition one, which meant that we had a round in the chamber of both our rifles and pistols with a magazine inserted. We were as ready as we could be to react to an attack. Then, one of the Triple Canopy security contractors who were with us yelled as he spun around and almost fell to the ground. "I've been hit—by a rock I think!" He had been standing right beside me, and we were now really on edge, and feeling very exposed. However, we could not determine the location from which the rock had been launched. It occurred to us, that if a man could hit us with a rock from a slingshot, it would be even easier to hit us using a rifle.

Minutes later, I felt the sting of impact as a rock struck me on the upper right bicep, an area not protected by any body armor. It hit me hard and it hurt like hell, but I was alright. Still, we saw no evidence of the attacker. Our adrenaline was racing by now as we anticipated an imminent attack; however, the attack never came. The large group of men down the alleyway dispersed and left. The shops and store fronts re-opened, and the women and children returned to the streets as if nothing out of the ordinary had happened. The Civil Affairs Team concluded its business, and we loaded up in our tactical vehicles, and returned to Camp Ramadi where we reported the strange incident. Later that day, the intelligence network "lit up" with reports of anticipated insurgent activity in Ramadi. The next day around noon, the infantry battalion in Ramadi was savagely attacked in ambush fashion in several areas--obviously a well-planned insurgent operation throughout the city. (We later learned that this was to be a three-day Jihad aimed at defeating the American occupiers and their Iraqi accomplices, the Iraqi government Security Forces.) The casualties were high on both sides as it was to be one of the bloodiest days and nights in the fight for Ramadi.

Late in the night or early morning, the bodies of the Marines who had been killed were brought to Camp Ramadi because a temporary morgue had been established there. My sergeant major, Sergeant Major Jan Miller, had heard rumors that one of the Marines who had been killed might be the brother of one of our Marines. He and I went down and helped to move the bodies, which were all in nylon "body bags," from the tactical vehicles to morgue. Nothing in my training or background could really have prepared me for the task of lifting and carrying the body of a recently killed Marine. It is a strangely bizarre feeling to bear the weight of a lifeless body, a body that only hours before was the living son of an American family. As we moved the bodies, Sergeant Major Miller and I knew what we had to do; we had to try to determine whether the rumor was true. By the light of a flashlight, we carefully unzipped each of the body bags to see if we could identify the man in question. We found him. To be sure, we found one of our staff non-commissioned officers who knew both the brothers, and he confirmed that the deceased Marine was indeed the younger brother of our Marine. We knew we had a responsibility to notify our Marine of his younger brother's death. Sergeant Major Miller and I spoke to Lieutenant Colonel Connally about the matter. Marines accept that they are in a dangerous business, but sometimes it becomes intimately personal, and this was one of those times. I could see the resolve forming in Lieutenant Colonel Connally's eyes. He spoke softly but firmly, "I will tell him. Send him to me in the morning. Have the Chaplain available to sit with us." Indeed, that is exactly how we handled the matter. We brought the young Marine to Lieutenant Colonel Connally, and he sat him down and broke the news to him in as compassionate a manner as any man could. Then Lieutenant Colonel Connally told our Marine that if the Marine wanted, he would arrange for him to serve as the escort for his brother—to take his brother home. Our Marine took the news of his brother's death as best he could, and I think that the offer to perform one last duty for his little brother somehow made the news just a little more bearable. He did in fact escort his brother home to his family, and he oversaw his brother's proper burial.

Lesson Learned

It is surely one of the toughest duties of a leader, to deliver tragic news such as the death of a family member. No death is easy to accept, but somehow this death in combat at the hands of the insurgency seemed to make it even more surreal and tragic. Lieutenant Colonel Connally was an exceptionally good battalion commander, but probably nothing in his training or educational background prepared him to deliver that news to his Marine that morning. He had to reach into his own character, his native humanity, and expose this very humanity to his Marine, as he related the tragedy with true compassion and sensitivity. By handling the matter as he did, Lieutenant Colonel Connally showed how deeply he cared for this Marine, and for all the rest of his Marines. I knew that leaders are sometimes called upon to deliver bad news to their people, but I learned that the way they do this is significantly important. Now, whenever I need to deliver bad news to someone on my team, I know I will do it in the same way that Lieutenant Colonel Connally did—with compassion and transparent, honest humanity. *I will tell him!*

Chapter Fifteen: "WHO Has Been Here?"

The Importance of Clear Communications: A Lesson from an "Abbott and Costello" Moment

When 3d Battalion, 11th Marines deployed to Iraq once again (2004), we went as Task Force Military Police. In addition to our primary mission of escorting logistics convoys throughout Al Anbar Province, we had the dubious assignment of running the Camp Ramadi Detention Facility, a rudimentary jail for housing captured enemy combatants. The Detention Facility itself was a relatively large square masonry structure with high walls and "rooms" that faced into an open center quadrangle. Camp Ramadi was an old Iraqi Army base, and this building was one of the existing structures, and given its configuration, I suspect that the Iraqi Army probably used it as a detention facility as well.

This was an active period in the insurgency, so there were plenty of suspects that required detention. The Camp Ramadi Detention Facility was one of only two such facilities in the Province that was authorized to hold any detainee for more than a couple days. Our mission there was to run the facility in a professional manner, and to ensure that all the detainees at our facility received proper and humane treatment. We managed the facility in a strict disciplined fashion as prescribed by the military's procedural manual for detention facilities. Since we were a Task Force, we had been augmented with a Military Police platoon, some of whom were activated Reserve Component Marines, and all of them were top-notch professionals. However, I do not think that any of our people, including the Military Police platoon, had any prior experience in operating a detention facility of any kind. We were the second unit to have this mission as the Army Division that 1st Marine Division relieved had established the facility during their deployment there in the Ramadi area. As with all military units that assume responsibility from another unit, part of our duty was to assess the established facility and in-place procedures, and to look for ways of improving both the facility and the manner in which we operated it. For instance, during our tenure, we installed showers and a laundry area. We kept strict logs on the daily schedule, and strict and detailed accountability of all the detainees' confiscated personal effects. On a routine basis, we had to transport a group of detainees from our facility to the main Detention Camp at Abu Ghraib. Even this required the exercise of strict procedures, and we performed that assignment with great professionalism.

Operating a Detention Facility on a combat deployment is not the role that most Marines, officer or enlisted, think about when they volunteer for service. However, it was a critically important function, and it had to be performed properly. We placed a young captain from the Military Police platoon in charge of the facility. He was just the right man to operate the facility as he was particularly smart, disciplined, and had great attention to detail. Moreover, he was even tempered and had a buoyant, motivated personality. Both the Battalion Commander and I made a point of visiting the facility frequently as part of our "leadership by walking around" tours. Our Officer-in-Charge (OIC) was always upbeat, as were all the Marines who served at the facility.

The Detention Facility had many visitors. For instance, one day some Iraqi media people came to visit. I doubt that they were allowed inside during the Saddam Hussain era. I was present when they visited, and we showed them everything at the facility, since there was nothing to hide. I do not know how these media people subsequently portrayed the Detention Facility in Iraqi media, but when they departed after their tour, they seemed to be satisfied.

One day, an Army general visited the facility. As our OIC walked him around the inside, the general said, "So captain, who has been here?" Our young captain replied, "No Sir, WHO has not been here yet." The general stopped walking, turned to the captain and said, "Captain, who has been here?" "No Sir, I am here all day most days, and we keep a log of visitors. I can say with confidence that WHO has not visited us yet." The general's frustration was obvious, and it was growing. He probably thought our captain was playing a game with him. "Captain, I am asking you, who--has--visited--you--here?!" Our captain then understood. "Oh Sir, I thought you were asking whether the World Health Organization (WHO) had already visited us. I'm sorry for my misunderstanding." The captain then answered the general's question.

Lesson Learned

We can all laugh at our captain's expense for his misunderstanding, but was it really his fault that he misunderstood? Communication requires two parties, and it is the responsibility of the communicator to effectively deliver their message in clear and unambiguous terms that the receiving party can understand. Communication is one of the most important leadership competencies, and leaders need to carefully monitor and examine without emotional bias how well their people are receiving the message that they as leaders are intending to deliver.

Chapter Sixteen: Press Ahead in the Face of Fear and Anxiety

In 2004 I was serving as a Battalion Executive Officer of an artillery battalion. Our unit deployed to western Iraq on our second deployment during my tenure with the unit. We left our artillery equipment behind and deployed as Task Force Military Police. Our Battalion Task Force was under the tactical control of an Army Brigade headquartered at Camp Ramadi, Iraq. Early in our deployment, I rode in a High-Mobility, Multi-Wheeled Vehicle (HMMWV) with the Brigade Executive Officer as we moved to a meeting at the nearby base of Al Taqaddum, about 30 kilometers to the east of Ramadi. As we reached the outskirts of Ramadi heading east on one of the main roads between the two camps, we observed a Marine infantry platoon out on foot patrol moving along the road. We passed on by, keeping our eyes on the road ahead of us, being particularly alert for signs of an improvised explosive device (IED). About 600 meters beyond the patrol, our driver executed an emergency braking maneuver because he had spotted a suspicious wire near the road. We were thankful that the wire turned out to be just roadside trash that is all too common and was not a part of an IED. About that time, while we were still standing outside our vehicles, we heard a loud explosion to our rear along the road over which we had just passed. We turned around to see the effects of the explosion, a tower of dust and debris. As the smoke cleared, we looked for the foot patrol, but we could not see anyone. We turned the convoy around and drove back to the site of the explosion which had detonated right in the middle of the road—just as the platoon of Marines was crossing over. One Marine was killed instantly, and another was horrifically wounded, including savage, potentially life-threatening wounds to his face. We called in a Medical Evacuation (MEDEVAC) aircraft to rush the wounded Marine to the nearest medical facility. When the MEDEVAC helicopter arrived, we quickly loaded the wounded Marine aboard, and we uploaded the body of the deceased Marine as well. I noted the location of the IED blast, right in the middle of the road in what was probably one of the ubiquitous potholes that littered the road all along its length. We had done all we could there, so we proceeded with our mission. My adrenaline was really pumping. Violence and death came so quickly, so suddenly, and it was a cold reminder of the kind of conflict in which we were engaged, and a warning against any complacency. Later, once I had calmed down, I thought that the insurgents could have targeted us instead of the foot patrol. I suspect that was indeed their original intent—

until they saw a target that was even less protected from the effects of their bomb.

A couple weeks later, I was once again in a convoy of HMMWV's traveling east between Ramadi and Taqqadum on the same road that we experienced the roadside bomb. This time, I was the vehicle commander sitting in the right front seat, and I had my handheld GPS out as I tracked our location. I told the Marines in the vehicle with me, "Gents, we're coming up on the location of the IED soon, and the insurgents have a tendency to use the same blast hole for another IED, so be ready." BOOM! The road in front of me erupted in thick black smoke and fragments of asphalt. It was a surreal feeling, as if it happened in slow motion. I am sure the blast was quite loud, but I do not remember the noise. In fact, since I had been anticipating this possibility, when it happened, it was almost like a scene out of Hollywood—and not real. Fortunately, the insurgents were off in their timing, and the explosion went off between my vehicle and the one in front of mine. The damage was limited to blowing out the back glass in the other vehicle (and causing minor cuts to the occupants). In my vehicle, we were fine. We stopped the convoy and searched for signs of the insurgents who detonated the bomb; but not surprisingly, we found only local families, and no one who was the likely antagonist. That was another of the frustrations with this conflict; facing the effects of violence, with no means of holding anyone accountable. Afterwards, once we arrived at our destination, and we started to come down from the adrenaline rush, I think we felt a mixture of anger and thankfulness. We were angry at the insurgents and our inability to prevent the strike, but we were thankful that our convoy had escaped serious injury. Strangely, I really did not feel any fear, either during the strike or afterward. I think we all felt an unusual sense of elation that can come from a "near-miss" experience like this. For the rest of our deployment, even though there was plenty of danger resulting from roadside bombs, as well as small arms attacks, we continued with our mission, albeit with the sober warning against any developed complacency.

Lesson Learned

I have heard it said that real courage is not the absence of fear, but rather the ability to press on in the face of fear and anxiety. That has proved true at a personal level for me and those with whom I served. Although the insurgents in the vicinity of Ramadi were waging an extremely active campaign of attrition at this time to make us pay a high price for our presence, we never allowed the threat of attack to dissuade us from performing our mission. However, we did seek to manage risk by taking prudent measures, such as varying our movement routes and times. We also started requesting a helicopter escort for many of our higher risk convoy escort missions, which lowered the incidence of small arms attack, and improved our ability to respond when we were attacked. The point is that we continued with our mission, even as we aggressively managed the risks. I believe the basic lesson from this experience applies in business as well as on the battlefield. Although the nature of the risks is different from what we faced in Iraq, every business leader will also have to face fears and anxieties, especially if they are trying something new, working in the dynamic environment of rapid change, or striving to stay ahead in a particularly competitive market (or all three). Leaders in all organizations, whether in business or government, will be forced to accept and manage risks —and will face fears and anxieties. Accept these natural emotions, manage the risks prudently, and *press on with the mission!*

Chapter Seventeen: Good People Rise to the Occasion

I was the Executive Officer for 3d Battalion, 11th Marines in 20003 when we received word that we would be deploying to Kuwait for staging in preparation for an assault into Iraq. We were in no way surprised by this as we had been anticipating this move for several months and had been earnestly training for it longer than that. One morning, as we made our final pre-deployment preparations, I was down at our Battalion Aid Station where our medical personnel worked, and our two Battalion Medical Officers pulled me aside to ask some questions. I could tell right away that they were both quite nervous about this impending deployment. They were asking me questions about where we would be living and our level of access to phones and internet so that they could stay in contact with their families back home. I chuckled a little as I explained our living arrangements at the austere desert camp we were going to be occupying. We would have little to no access to phones of any kind, and no access to the internet. We would be forced to rely on the old-fashioned method of communication—letters. I could tell that communication with home was only one of their concerns, and probably not the main one. They were plainly anxious about their role in combat operations and the level of danger they would be facing.

During my long career, I have seen that the military has some of the finest health care professionals. Many doctors are initially drawn to the military for financial reasons because the military, in many cases, can defray the high costs of medical education in exchange for terms of military service. During times of peace, this may seem like a relatively low risk option, but during times of conflict, the military deploys its medical teams alongside or integrated with its combat units. I suspect that neither of our two Battalion Medical Officers had anticipated being required to deploy in support of combat operations, at least not something like this. One of them even wrote his congressman trying to look for ways to avoid having to deploy with us.

Once we deployed to Kuwait, neither of these two doctors were any less anxious about their situation. As an artillery unit, we would be in direct support of the infantry, and there would be no denying the personal danger that we all would face. Eventually, we received our orders to proceed to our final pre-assault positions and prepare to move forward in the assault. For the Marines, this was an exciting time, because we were doing what we had been training for so long to do. On schedule we fired our preparation fires and then moved forward to keep up with the advancing maneuver element.

Several days into this operation, we faced something for which we could never have trained; a monstrous sandstorm. Sandstorms are rather common in the arid Middle East, but this was no "ordinary" sandstorm. The day was almost turned to night and the night became pitch black, as if we were inside a cave. I could not see my hand in front of my face. Although our forward motion was temporarily halted, our battalion continued to provide artillery fires in support of the infantry. One night some of our Marines were conducting a local security patrol around the unit's perimeter when one of the Marines was shot in the upper chest. The wounded Marine was evacuated to the Battalion Aid Station for evaluation and treatment. I was back there with the team when the unit brought in the wounded Marine. The unit Corpsman (what the Marine Corps calls our Navy medics) told us that the round appeared to have pieced the chest below the shoulder, and it might be not be immediately life threatening. One of our doctors, the one who had written his congressman and showed, up to that point, the greatest level of personal anxiety, took the wounded Marine into the back of the ambulance vehicle to examine him. After a short while, he came out and told me, "Sir, I believe that the round angled down and pieced his lung. He is now bleeding out internally, and we need to get him to a surgeon as fast as we are able." He spoke confidently, with calmness and firmness. Was this the same man who earlier had shown such nervousness? Now he was in his element, and despite the horrible conditions, he was doing what he had been trained to do, and without the paralysis of fear. I grabbed our Battalion Motor Transport Officer and gave him the simplest of instructions. "I need you to escort this wounded Marine to the Surgical Station that has been established just off the road three kilometers to our north." The Motor Transport Officer loaded the wounded Marine up and drove off in the pitch black. After what seemed the longest time, he radioed me and told me he had not located the Surgical Station. What should he do? I knew that time was not on our side, and if he could not find the Surgical Station to our north, I would be forced to send him over six kilometers south to where another Surgical Station was located. What should I do? What instructions should I give him? I took a deep breath and as I decided that I had to send him to the south, the Motor Transport Officer radioed that he just found the Surgical Station!

After taking the wounded Marine in for evaluation and treatment, the surgeons told our Motor Transport Officer that our Marine would not have lasted even another 30 minutes had he not received medical intervention. I could see that if I had sent them to the other Surgical Station, the Marine would likely have died in transit. As it was, the wounded Marine was evacuated and he survived the experience—thanks to the medical judgment of our Battalion Medical Officer who rose to the occasion, despite his personal anxieties.

Lesson Learned

If we as leaders are not careful, we can overlook great talent and ability among our teams. We must remain open to the possibility that some of our teammates may be exactly the right man or woman for a particular project or circumstance, perhaps something that has not yet appeared in our view. Our Battalion Medical Officer developed a certain kind of bravery once he was challenged with something for which he was prepared to perform. In fact, he was indeed the only one who could perform the critical evaluation of the wounded Marine and knowing that gave him purpose. Suddenly, he was no longer concerned about himself, but instead was able to focus his concern on others. I was reminded that good people rise to the occasion, and it was part of my role as a leader to help my teammates understand their purpose on the team, and to be ever vigilant for the opportunity to match the right person to the task for which they are uniquely skilled and prepared to perform.

Chapter Eighteen: Be Sensitive to Emergent Organizational Requirements

In 2006 I was serving at the Marine Corps Combat Development Command at Quantico, Virginia in the Concepts and Plans Division. Our Branch was busy writing concepts for the future needs of the Marine Corps. One day one of my colleagues received an email from his brother, a Marine officer who was serving with a unit deployed to Afghanistan. In the email, my colleague's brother noted that the Marines were experiencing a great deal of physical difficulty and hardship as they conducted foot patrols carrying all their heavy gear across the hilly terrain of Afghanistan. My colleague's brother felt that the Marine Corps should make a concerted effort to lighten the load that Marines are forced to carry, because it was proving too physically taxing to chase a lightly-equipped enemy who could move quicker and easier. Both my colleague and I agreed with this assessment as it was not really a new problem. The load requirements that we placed on Marines seemed to only increase over time. However, I thought that perhaps there is something more here. We could champion the initiative to use technological advances to lighten the load we required Marines to bear, but that change would take years. What other ways could we attack this problem? If we could not immediately make a significant reduction in the load, perhaps we could find ways to better prepare the Marines to carry the load, and to better perform other combat duties that required strength and endurance. With this as my working thesis, I set about researching physical training regimes and comparing them to what we were already doing.

I spent months studying the problem, and I found from my research that although the Marine Corps valued physical fitness generally, only one component of fitness, aerobic endurance, was being prioritized. There was little enterprise-wide effort to view Marines as professional athletes that required deliberate training for strength, anaerobic endurance, power, and agility. Following my research, I wrote the Marine Corps Concept for Functional Fitness. Change is difficult, but sometimes you get lucky and the timing will be right for change. That was the case with the functional fitness initiative. A grass roots swell began, much of it fueled by Marines returning from Iraq and Afghanistan who had experienced the physical stressors of combat, but felt that we were not doing enough, in the corporate sense, to intentionally prepare our troops for the physical demands we experienced. The Marine Corps responded by revamping the physical fitness program and adopting many of the initiatives proposed in the Concept. Today, the Marine Corps openly talks of Marines as professional athletes. Meal choices in the dining facilities are being adjusted with performance in mind. Access to sports medicine providers has radically improved. A cadre of functional fitness trainers is being created and pushed down to the unit level. Even the Fitness Test itself has been updated to capture functional fitness better. The net effect is that the Marine Corps now has stronger, more resilient Marines who are better able to perform their physical tasks, especially the demanding ones they face in a combat environment. The Marine Corps is still working to lighten the combat load.

Lesson Learned

What began as an email note between two brothers ultimately led to a change affecting the entire Marine Corps in large and meaningful ways. I learned first-hand how difficult it was to advocate for enterprise-wide changes. Similarly, I learned the importance of organizational agility, which demanded that we remain sensitive to emergent organizational requirements. In many cases, experiences in recent combat operations brought forth a new awareness and prioritization of operational needs. That observation is exemplified by the rush to develop vehicles that could better survive the effects of improvised explosive devices and by the propagation of personal body armor and flame-retardant clothing. Business leaders do not face an enemy that eludes them or that injures or kills their people, but they do face threats of another kind. Businesses need to evolve rapidly ahead of their dynamic environments if they are to survive and thrive. Sometimes that change requirement may begin at the grass roots level with a simple observation. Leaders in all organizations, private and public, benefit from creating a culture that is sensitive to new ideas and new requirements. *Do you have a need akin to the Marine Corps' experience with the Concept for Functional Fitness, and is your corporate culture sensitive to emergent requirements, even those that emanate from the grass roots level?*

Chapter Nineteen: "Sir, I Have an Idea."

Using All the Tools at Your Disposal

In 2007 I took command of 3d Battalion, 10th Marines, at Camp Lejeune, a North Carolina-based artillery battalion. I knew when I assumed command that my previous experiences in provisional infantry and military police work would be useful, because we were re-designated as Task Force Military Police for our upcoming combat deployment to Iraq. We assigned one of my organic batteries to operate the Camp Falluja Detention Facility, one battery worked convoy escort based out of Camp Falluja, and another organic battery worked convoy escort based out of Al Asad (further west in Al Anbar Province). In addition, we attached an active duty military police company, which operated out of Camp Ramadi, and a reserve military police company, which we tasked with running the border entry points out west at Walid (Syrian border) and Trebil (Jordanian border). We also gained a detachment of military working dogs and dog handlers. The dog handlers were both Marines and Sailors, and we had both male and female dog handlers. In fact, we were one of the first combat arms units to deploy with females integrated in our combat arms unit. Our battalion adjutant was a female officer, and she served superbly in combat operations. The Task Force was

100

literally spread out across the expanse of Al Anbar. My Task Force headquarters was at Al Asad, a large logistics base aboard a former Iraqi air base in the center of Al Anbar.

The progress in the fight against the Sunni insurgency in Al Anbar was obvious by the time we deployed there in 2008. Compared to the "Wild West" environment that I saw in 2004, the situation in the spring of 2008 was showing signs of stability and some return to normality. However, we knew we had to remain vigilant and disciplined. We knew that the enemy could exploit any complacency on our part.

One night we received reports that one of the new Forward Operating Bases recently erected near Camp Fallujah had come under ground attack. There was a tall concrete wall around the circumference of the small base with guard towers integrated into the wall network. Somehow, some insurgents had apparently scaled the wall at a point that had limited observation. They gained access using a rope ladder, and once inside, they got into a gunfight with the Marine sentries in the towers—firing up at the Marine sentries from the ground! Then, after creating a great deal of havoc, the insurgents (number unknown) managed to leave the compound in the same manner they entered, via their rope ladders, which they left behind. Fortunately, there were no casualties.

The next day, the Commanding General had all of his commanders on a video teleconference. I had never seen him as frustrated and angry as he was then. He wanted answers. How did this happen, and what could we do about it? How could we ensure it never, ever happened again? He was not so much chastising his commanders as he was genuinely searching out answers, and no one was able to provide him anything satisfactory in the way of a response. The commander who owned the Forward Operating Base clearly did not feel comfortable having the Commanding General looking so closely into his affairs; nevertheless, he was sufficiently chagrined with the humiliating incident that he chose to say very little. The video tele-conference ended with the Commanding General asking for us to get back to him with a plan to deal with this security shortfall.

After I signed off from the call, I thought about the assets I had, and how we might be able to help. I thought about our process of performing Sensitive Site Exploitation at the point of a crime, and I imagined that there might be evidence at the scene that we could exploit for intelligence purposes. I called the Commanding General on his secure phone. "Sir, I have an idea. We have Military Working Dog teams, and we have the capability of using the dogs to potentially pick up the scent and track the insurgents. Perhaps we can learn more about how the enemy was able to approach an apparent blind spot in the outpost's defensive wall unobserved and scale the wall." The General loved the idea and ordered me to see to it. Now my only problem was transporting a dog and handler team from out west where the tracking dog was based over to this small base near Fallujah. We decided that it had to be performed via helicopter transport, so we submitted the request. Unfortunately, due to bad weather and some scheduling complications related to the prioritization of aircraft, I was not able to get my tracking dog and handler to the scene until a couple days later. When they finally arrived, the trail was cold, and the scene where the insurgents gained access had been sufficiently disturbed that we were not able to accomplish much in the way of intelligence gathering. Needless to say, I was frustrated at the missed opportunity to gain some important intelligence on the enemy and to showcase our working dogs' value to the division. Fortunately, the enemy never attempted to scale the wall again.

Lesson Learned

Although our response to the insurgent infiltration did not prove productive as I had hoped, I nonetheless believe that it was a good idea. To put it bluntly, we as leaders within the division were initially thinking too linearly when we considered our options. Military units in combat are not the only ones guilty of this tendency to view the problem and its solution simplistically. Most organizations struggle with solving complex problems, and like the military, find it difficult to maximize the effectiveness of the tools and resources they have at their disposal. To do this well, organizations require agility; and often inertia and bureaucracy interfere with an organization's ability to swiftly re-prioritize assets and pivot sharply to seize a fleeting opportunity. By the time the assets are brought to bear, the "trail is cold," and the opportunity lost. Although it is best that organizations take measures to prevent their "enemy from scaling their security wall" (whatever their organizational equivalent of that may be), the next best thing is to respond with dexterity when the "enemy" surprises them, and that will require the consideration of all the tools that are reasonably at the organization's disposal.

Chapter Twenty: Pause Before Rendering Judgment

The Case of the Missing Trailer

Early in my tenure as an artillery battalion commander, I experienced my first case of executive dismay; the kind that makes you scratch your head and ask aloud, "How could that happen?" Units are required to conduct regular inventories on all their assigned equipment, and for an artillery battalion, that is a rather involved process, because these units have a great deal of equipment for which they are responsible. One morning I overheard part of a conversation between my Battalion Executive Officer, Major Todd Peery and our Battalion Supply Officer. The gist of the conversation was that we were apparently "missing" a trailer for a High Mobility Multi-Wheeled Vehicle (HMMWV). The Supply Officer was in the process of explaining that during a routine inventory inspection, the team down in the motor pool (where we kept all our vehicles and associated equipment) had been unable to locate or account for a trailer associated with one of our HMMWVs. The value of the missing trailer was such that an investigation was required. At that point in my career, I had been in the Marine Corps just over 19 years. At one point in my career I thought I had "seen it all," but I discovered as a battalion commander that, no, I had not seen it all. I had a feeling that this was going to be one of those occasions.

Major Peery and I quizzed the Supply Officer for the relevant facts. Had the trailer been evacuated for maintenance? Had the trailer been loaned out to another unit? Had the trailer been removed from the supply account, and the inventory list simply did not reflect the update? The Supply Officer answered "no" to all our obvious questions. Now I started getting concerned. I said, "A HMMWV trailer does not just get up and roll itself out of the motor pool!" The Supply Officer had no answers beyond a confirmation that the trailer was accounted for on the previous inventory, so whoever "took" it, must have done so recently. The Supply Officer reiterated his point about an investigation being required. I said, "Okay, XO, let's assign an investigating officer. This may require some detective work."

Major Peery selected Lieutenant Courtney Boston, one of our sharpest young officers, to conduct this sensitive investigation—the case of the missing trailer. Frankly, I was not sure how I would be able to explain this to my boss, the Regimental Commander. I was, however, sure that it would be embarrassing when I tried. Major Peery brought Lieutenant Boston in and explained the case to him based on the facts as we knew them. I almost felt embarrassed to admit to our own investigating officer that we were unable to keep our trailers from "walking off." I hoped that Lieutenant Boston would be thorough in his pursuit of the facts. Major Peery asked Lieutenant Boston to keep him apprised of the progress of the investigation and sent him off to begin.

Less than a day later, Lieutenant Boston returned to speak with Major Peery. He said that he had located the trailer. Major Peery asked him, "Where did you find it?" Lieutenant Boston had a "You are not going to believe this" look on his face, so I assumed that this should be an interesting story. He replied, "Sir, I found the trailer parked in the battalion motor pool—it was there all the time!" Apparently, someone had moved the trailer to a different section of the motor pool area (which was not that large), so when the inventory was performed, there was confusion. At first, I was torn between relief and incredulity, but after I recovered myself, I decided that this embarrassing episode had a positive ending. Major Peery and I observed that Lieutenant Boston concluded his investigation about the fastest we had ever seen an investigation conducted! Fortunately, this one turned out well; though it did elicit newfound concerns on my part over our accountability procedures down in the motor pool.

Lesson Learned

Many tactical leaders have learned the hard way that initial reports are often wrong or missing critical facts. For that reason, seasoned leaders discipline themselves to "take a deep breath" when they first hear of an incident, and probe for additional information before reacting or rendering a decision. The case of the "missing" HMMWV trailer was a reminder for me that often things are not as they are first reported to be, and that there is usually more to the story, and I needed to exercise some patience while our team looked into the matter. Leaders in business and in the public sector will also hear bad news, and your natural instinct will be to immediately react, often in frustration. My advice is to remember the case of the "missing" HMMWV trailer and be patient while your team delves into the matter at hand. *After all, your trailer may still be in your own motor pool!*

Chapter Twenty-one: Dealing with Bad News

In general, people do not like to give their boss bad news. They are afraid of how their boss will react, and they are afraid of the consequences, particularly if the bad news reflects poorly on their work performance. People are afraid that their boss will associate the bad news with something that they, the bearer of the bad news, did or failed to do, with possible career implications either way. Even when the bad news involves something with no obvious performance issues, people tend to avoid being the person who put their boss in a bad mood.

The problem with this avoidance tendency is that bosses really need to hear the bad news; and they need to hear it in a timely manner. Bosses need the unvarnished truth—all the time. Leaders can quickly find themselves at variance with the reality of a situation if they are not in receipt of all the relevant facts of a case. Leaders who lack good situational awareness will tend to make poor decisions and produce inaccurate reports to their higher headquarters. As the old saying goes, "Bad news does not get better with time." Leaders are much more likely to take prudent actions or to react in a more productive fashion if they learn early of a bad situation.

So if leaders know that they need to hear bad news early, why is it so common for these same leaders to react in a fashion which deters people from actually bringing them the bad news? Why do leaders react angrily at the person delivering the message? Essentially, the leader who "blows up" when one of their people present them with bad news is sending a not too subtle signal that they do not want to hear bad news. That leader is discouraging the very behavior which they absolutely need to encourage.

In 2007, when I was the Commander of Third Battalion, Tenth Marines, I had a superb Senior Enlisted Advisor in the person of Sergeant Major Ray Mackey. Ray was an experienced sergeant major, and I was not the first commander with whom he served. Ray was an infantryman by background, and we were fortunate to have him in the artillery community. Somewhere in his background he learned the importance of bringing unsavory news to the boss as soon as he could, and presenting it in a manner in which the commander could absorb and respond productively. Sergeant Major Mackey would come into my office, and with a bit of homespun humor say, "Sir, what had happened was..." I knew then that I needed to sit down, take a deep breath, and just "drink it in." Artillery battalions have a high percentage of energetic, young men who are still in the stage of development in which wisdom has not been experientially acquired. Many are less than a year out of high school. As a commander, I had to accept that they were going to make some mistakes. Some were going to display lapses in judgment that might land them in trouble, and in some cases I was forced to take corrective disciplinary action. But regardless of the news, I knew I needed to hear it, and if I had not already heard it from another source, at least I could hear it from Sergeant Major Mackey.

While an artillery battalion may have a relatively high number of disciplinary infractions, in most respects, it is not so unique from other kinds of organizations in terms of the interpersonal dynamics. Every leader needs to have at least one Sergeant Major Mackey, the person who has complete access to the boss, and who has developed a rapport with the boss for delivering news, good or bad, with complete authenticity and candor. Leaders would do well to intentionally foster that kind of a relationship with someone that they trust, so that behind closed doors, that person can present them with news that might cause the leader to wince. However, the onus is on the leader to discipline their emotions to the point that they are always ready to receive undesirable news. A leader cannot afford to be the sort for whom his or her people need to "wait until the time is right" in order to deliver bad news. Sometimes there is a time-sensitive component with a problem, and any postponement in learning of the situation only results in a delayed, and perhaps less effective or relevant response.

Lesson Learned

While it is best that leaders are even-tempered, even if they are not, all leaders should be self-aware of how they receive undesirable news from their team. It is very much in the best interests of the organization and of the individual leader that he or she receives bad news at the earliest practical moment, and with the least filtration. Leaders make the best decisions when they receive the unadulterated truth—in a time-sensitive fashion. This is true in the military, but it is equally true in business. *Learn to react calmly to bad news and find your own Sergeant Major Mackey.*

Chapter Twenty-two: Holding People Accountable

As an artillery battalion commander, I was assigned the mission of forming Task Force Military Police from my battalion, with the additions of two other companies and various other individual augmentees. I transformed my 580-man battalion into a 1000-man Task Force, and we deployed to Al Anbar Province, Iraq in 2008.

I had a great team of leaders, both on my Task Force staff, and at the individual battery/company level. We were required to operate across the entirety of the Al Anbar Province, and that would simply not have been possible were it not for decentralized command and control performed by leaders I knew and trusted. Although I believed in "leadership by walking around," or in this case, driving and flying around, I could not possibly see everything that was going on with my Task Force. I published standards of conduct early in our combat deployment and expected all my subordinate leaders to enforce those standards of conduct. However, inevitably in a unit that large and that spread out, there were going to be violations of our published rules.

About mid-way through our deployment, I was apprised of just such a violation. We had been tasked with an unusual mission, to escort the "Mother of All Generators" or MOAG for short, from the Iraqi border with Jordan to a power plant north of Baghdad. This was an enormous generator. The relatively narrow roads combined with the tremendous weight of the MOAG required the team to drive very slowly—often only 5 miles per hour—all day long. The mission took over 10 days to execute, and it was carried out by a lieutenant and his security platoon. About halfway through the mission, a few of the Marines were apparently getting bored. One morning before the platoon started the day's movement, some of the Marines noticed that they were near an Iraqi farm and they saw a lone cow in a field. One of the Marines dared another to go over to the cow and punch it. One of the corporals, a squad leader, said, "Hold it a minute so I can get my video camera out." The Marine who had been dared walked out into the field, approached the cow, and then after pausing to make sure it was being filmed, punched the cow. I learned of the incident days later after the platoon had otherwise successfully completed the MOAG mission and returned to their Forward Operating Base at Camp Ramadi. One of the Staff non-commissioned officers saw the video and confiscated it. In it, the corporal, can be heard saying, "This is what happens when you leave Marines by themselves for such a long and boring mission." Of course, the corporal was the young leader who should have been enforcing the rule I passed to leave all cameras and video recorders back at the base.

I made a special trip from our headquarters at Al Asad to Camp Ramadi (about a three-hour movement one direction) just to discipline the Marines involved in this incident. The Marine who punched the cow accepted his punishment as if he received what he deserved. I reduced him in rank and put an adverse remark in his record. However, the corporal was rather indignant when I punished him. When I reminded him that he had disobeyed an order to not take video recorders or cameras on a mission he responded, "But sir, everyone does it!" I responded that I could not speak for who was or was not obeying my order, but that as a corporal of Marines, I expected him to obey my orders and to enforce the orders. Moreover, by failing to intervene and even by recording the incident, he was complicit in the offense of punching an Iraqi farmer's cow, which we could both agree was extremely poor judgment on his part. I told him, "You did not act like a corporal when I needed you to; therefore, you are no longer a corporal." He surrendered his hard-earned chevrons to the Sergeant Major. I hope that he learned an important lesson that day, that leaders enforce the standards—and that ultimately, leaders hold their people accountable.

Lesson Learned

The military relies a great deal on subordinate leaders enforcing the standards of discipline, especially in combat where the stakes are so incredibly high for any lapse in discipline. When a team member shows a lapse in judgment, they should be held to account, even if that simply amounts to counselling or a verbal rebuke. This is true in all kinds of organizations, not just the military. This intervention can be handled with discretion and in an instructive manner, so that the experience is not demeaning or embarrassing for the person being counselled. The point is that team members need to know that they will be held accountable for their behavior, and that their leaders will be fair and consistent with them, even during the process of counselling or admonishing them.

Chapter Twenty-three: A Leader's Responsibility

I remember a story that General Joe Dunford, USMC once told a group of commanders. He related an experience he had when he was an infantry battalion commander. One of the Marines in the battalion had committed an offense for which his leadership had charged him with a breach of the Uniform Code of Military Justice. Now he, the Battalion Commander, was seeing the Marine at "Office Hours." General Dunford said that before the Marine entered the room, he had the Marine's leaders in front of him as he reviewed the charges. General Dunford turned to the Marine's platoon commander and said, "Lieutenant, may I please see your Platoon Commander's Notebook?" The Platoon Commander's Notebook is simply a notebook that most leaders at the platoon level kept on their Marines to document performance and counselling. The lieutenant, quite embarrassed, admitted that he did not keep a Platoon Commander's Notebook. General Dunford queried him on whether he, the Platoon Commander, understood that this was one of his expectations of all the platoon commanders in the battalion. The Platoon Commander seemed confused on this point. Additionally, both he and the Company

Commander were unable to show evidence that they had previously counselled this Marine on any previous instances of his offense. Ultimately, General Dunford sent the company leadership away without conducting non-judicial punishment.

Lesson Learned

What is to be learned from this story that General Dunford related? At the time that I first heard it, I reasoned that he was teaching his platoon commanders that they needed to meet his expectations for keeping records of their Marines' performance and of their counselling sessions. I have no doubt that the admonished lieutenant spread the word that the boss was quite serious about all of them keeping good Platoon Commander's Notebooks! But as I have reflected on this story over the years, and served as a commander myself, I believe there was a bigger lesson that General Dunford was teaching his officers. I believe that then Lieutenant Colonel Dunford was teaching his leaders that he expected more from *them*. He expected them to coach, counsel, teach, and mentor their Marines, not just to punish them for their infractions of the rules. Lieutenant Colonel Dunford was not disputing that the Marine was guilty of the infraction for which he had been charged, nor was he indicating that it was in any way inappropriate that the matter had been referred up to his level. His real point, I believe, was that long before this infraction resulted in this Marine standing before his Battalion Commander, there were many other leaders who should have intervened in his discipline development, and that the Platoon Commander's Notebook was really just an artifact to attest to the level of interest that leaders were showing in this young man's maturing process. I think in effect, General Dunford was saying, I expect you to care for your people and for their professional development. Show me evidence of that. I believe *he was reminding them of their responsibility as leaders*, one that should precede any disciplinary action. Business leaders may not have similar disciplinary responsibilities as military leaders do; however, they do have a responsibility to help their people develop to the point that they are regularly meeting the leader's expectations for workplace behavior and job performance. *Remember the lesson of the Platoon Commanders' Notebook.*

Chapter Twenty-four: Maintaining Your Sense of Humor

In 2007 I was a Task Force commander with my unit spread out across Al Anbar Province, and I spent quite a bit of time on the roads of western Iraq. One day we were in our small security convoy heading west between Camp Fallujah and Camp Ramadi when we began to cross the Ramadi Bridge; which I knew from a previous tour to be a dangerous area. Our lead vehicle had a mine-roller in front, and as the vehicle was almost over the bridge, the mine-roller collapsed and would not roll forward. Now the rest of the vehicles were stuck on the bridge, not a place I wanted to stay, especially in broad daylight. My Sergeant Major, Sergeant Major Ray Mackey had an idea. Perhaps we could winch the vehicle and damaged plow out of the way. He reached down and grabbed the winch hook from our vehicle and yelled at our driver to play out some slack. Unfortunately, our driver was not very familiar with the operation of the winch, and rather than play out slack, he hit the switch to retract the cable. I watched in horror as Sergeant Major Mackey's hand was pulled into the winch! He was able to pull it free, but not before the winch had crushed some of his fingers.

Now I had a Medical Evacuation to accomplish...of my own Sergeant Major. Fortunately, the Camp Ramadi gate was only about one kilometer away. I loaded Sergeant Major Mackey into my vehicle, which we had managed to get around the lead vehicle with the broken winch, and we drove quickly for Camp Ramadi. At the gate, the guard ordered us to dismount for weapons clearing. I stuck my head out my window and yelled at him, "I have an emergency medevac. I need to get my casualty to Charlie Med as fast as I can!" The guard jumped out of the way and motioned us through. Having served at Camp Ramadi before, I knew where the medical area was located, and we quickly drove there. Once we arrived, I got Sergeant Major Mackey out of the vehicle, threw his good arm over my shoulder, and helped him into the clinic. The medical team rushed him into immediate surgery in an effort to save as much of his hand as they could. After a couple hours, the medical team came out and informed me that they had done as much as they could, and were going to fly him to Al Asad, where the actual hospital was located. Once the helicopter was airborne, we rallied our convoy and drove to Al Asad ourselves, as that is where our Task Force Headquarters was based. It was a long drive as I worried about my Sergeant Major. Once I arrived at Al Asad, I immediately went to check on him. Once he came out of surgery, he looked up at me and said, "Sir, I got the easy ride home—and beat you!"

Fortunately, the medical team at Camp Ramadi had done everything right. The best hand surgeon in Iraq just happened to be there at Camp Ramadi. He probably saved Sergeant Major Mackey's hand. At Al Asad hospital, the doctors finished the work. Sergeant Major Mackey lost half of his trigger finger, but that was all. He was confined to the hospital bed for a couple weeks to recover, and to allow the medical staff to change the dressings and keep the wound clean as it started to heal.

One day when I went to visit him in the hospital Sergeant Major Mackey proudly announced, "Sir, Lieutenant Dan was here. You just missed him!" "What are you talking about Sergeant Major." "Sir, Lieutenant Dan, you know, the guy in Forrest Gump. He came by to visit us here." Sergeant Major Mackey had a big smile on his face, and I knew he was going to be fine. I had not heard that Gary Sinise was going to be there to visit our wounded warriors, but I was glad he did. It was a classy move. Sergeant Major Mackey was tough—and chose to stay with the Task Force on that deployment. In fact, it was not long before he was back out on the road with us--after he taught himself to shoot with his middle finger!

Lesson Learned

Sergeant Major Mackey was strong and unflappable. He also had a great sense of humor, and he used it during tense situations to help others stay calm. He taught me that lesson, that it is important for leaders to maintain their sense of humor, especially in difficult circumstances. If you can communicate emotional strength and stability in the midst of tough times, you may be able to help others deal calmly with the situation as well. Sergeant Major Mackey's positive attitude was absolutely infectious, even when he was so obviously in pain. In this sense, he demonstrated his selfless nature, a quality I greatly admired and sought to emulate. Leaders in all kinds of organizations should remember this simple lesson—that it is important to maintain your sense of humor during times of stress. *If you show calmness and stability, you can help your team cope with stressful circumstances.*

Chapter Twenty-five: Mental Imaging for Leaders

When I was a member of 3d Battalion, 11th Marines, I was a part of the famous 1st Marine Division then commanded by Major General James Mattis. I came to believe that General Mattis was one of the most brilliant leaders I had ever known. Under his leadership, the division became combat ready in a way that I had never experienced. General Mattis understood men and war, and part of his unique genius was in preparing men and women for the challenges of war, many of which are mental.

Before our second deployment to Iraq, General Mattis commissioned the staff to create a brief to be given to all hands that explained every step in our deploying process from the point we were in at home station, to the point we would be once we arrived at our respective areas of operation. The intent was to walk every member of the division through what they could expect to experience. General Mattis wanted to use the process of "mental imaging" to help his team visualize what they would be doing before they actually did it. I thought this was brilliant and sought to use it myself when I took command.

I was first introduced to the concept of mental management when I was being coached in advanced marksmanship techniques almost 25 years ago. Mental management taught me to manage my performance in my mind in a very deliberate fashion. Using metal management, I went through the steps of the shot so that I had already fired an accurate shot before I actually pulled the trigger. During live fire, if a shot did not go where I wanted it, using mental management I "called" my shot and asked myself what I did incorrectly. I told myself what adjustment I needed to make for the next shot. Then I said to myself, "I shoot black!"

As a commander of Marines, I learned that it was useful, especially before our combat deployment, to "image" my Marines through events as I anticipated them occurring. Everyone has fears and anxieties about the future, consciously or subconsciously. Often these anxieties revolve around how they will perform in a tough and stressful circumstance. Will they perform to expectations? Will they measure up and show courage in the face of difficulty? What kind of living conditions should they expect? I started using a form of General Mattis' technique of mental imaging to walk my Marines through the future as I saw it unfolding. My intent was to paint a mental picture of the future for my Marines. In this way, they had an image (a positive one) of the future with them in it. We know that when someone has been in a circumstance before, they are often less anxious about going into it. The virtual tour that I gave them was aimed at allowing my Marines to "be there" before they physically arrived.

Lesson Learned

I learned the effectiveness of mental imaging prior to an operation or major event. Over time, I also learned to use a form of it in less demanding or challenging circumstances when I wanted to help all of our team "see" the situation similarly, as if they had already experienced it before. I believe this technique has utility for leaders in all types of organizations, including business and government. The point is to create a mental image of the future that involves the accomplishment of a desired goal by giving your team a virtual tour leading to the end-state. In most cases, the more participatory the leader makes the experience with his or her team, the more the individual team members are likely to internalize the image and benefit from the exercise. *Consider ways that you might be able to use mental imaging with your team.*

Chapter Twenty-six: Developing Resiliency

After my time as an artillery battalion commander, I was promoted and transferred to Headquarters Marine Corps, Plans, Policies and Operations Directorate at the Pentagon. That represented an abrupt move and change of focus from the tactical to the strategic level. However, with the then ongoing conflicts in both Iraq and Afghanistan, our attention was never too far from what our Marines were doing on the ground in active combat zones.

One day in late December 2010, one of our senior enlisted men came to my office and showed me a casualty report. During that period, casualties, unfortunately, were all too common; however, this report caught his eye because the service member was very seriously injured, and because the Marine was an E-9, the senior enlisted rank. "Sir, do you know this man?" I took the paper from his hand, and as I looked down at the words, it felt like my heart skipped a beat and I had trouble breathing. The report read Mackey, Raymond, E-9. That was Sergeant Major Ray Mackey—my former Sergeant Major, and my friend! I read the incident summary. The gist of the report was that Sergeant Major Mackey had been out with on the Battalion's foot-mobile security patrols in Afghanistan, when the patrol was attacked with an improvised explosive device (IED).

Apparently, Sergeant Major Mackey had been right next to the IED when the insurgents activated the explosive. The blast amputated both his legs above the knees. Somehow, the Marines and the Navy Corpsman with the patrol managed to stop the bleeding and get him on a Medical Evacuation helicopter. Once he had been initially stabilized in a hospital in Afghanistan, he was flown to Germany, and then on to Walter Reed Hospital in Washington DC, our premier military medical treatment facility. He lived.

My wife, Rhonda, and I drove up to Walter Reed to visit him soon after he arrived. When we got to his room, his wife, Vicki, was there by his bedside. She was a real trooper, and she was holding up amazingly well. As we talked, Ray began to regain consciousness. (He had been very heavily sedated.) As he opened his eyes, he looked up at me. "Sir, am I in Louisiana?" "No Ray, you are at Walter Reed in DC." He paused as this news sunk in. He told us that he did not remember even being at the hospital in Germany. He then began relating some of what happened in the attack. His memory was amazingly lucid. He even remembered the Marines loading him aboard the helicopter. He knew he had lost most of his legs. The medical staff later told me that the surgeons might have to remove even more flesh from his legs as they cleaned up the wound in order to prevent gangrene from setting in, a real concern in severe cases like this.

Sergeant Major Mackey had the dubious distinction of being the senior enlisted man of any service that had been grievously wounded to this degree in either Afghanistan or Iraq—and to have survived. Now came the hard part. The doctors saved as much of his upper legs as they could through many, many surgeries. Ray began the long battle of rehabilitation, and that would prove to be the most difficult fight that this old warrior had ever endured. He was not alone. In fact, he represented the many warriors who came to Walter Reed from the battlefields of Iraq and Afghanistan with indescribable wounds—wounds that would surely have proved fatal in any previous era of combat. To say that their injuries were "life altering" would be a gross understatement; but though their physical injuries were obvious enough to see, these wounded warriors, like Ray Mackey, endured psychological wounds that were just as deep and debilitating. The long, painful, and often lonely road to recovery to a state of "new normal" is something that only these wounded warriors can fully understand and appreciate. We may be able to sympathize with them, but Ray could truly empathize. However, this is not a story of defeat, but of victory. Ray Mackey is one tough Marine, and with

Vicki's help, and the support of his many friends and supporters, Ray recovered and returned to his home in North Carolina.

Today, Ray is an advocate for wounded warriors and a motivational speaker. Each December he celebrates his "Alive Day" to commemorate another year he has on this earth. At the time of this writing, he is celebrating his ninth "Alive Day." Resiliency is defined as the ability to cope with significant stressors and to rebound, to bend and snap back instead of breaking. From my vantage point, Sergeant Major Ray Mackey personifies this concept of resiliency at the most human level. Despite his injury and the disability that he lives with every day, Ray remains the positive, upbeat man he has always been, and inspires others with his example. Moreover, he has a new voice in that he can connect with many other wounded warriors, most of whom are quite young and inexperienced in life, in a way that no one else ever could.

Lesson Learned

I relate this story because I believe it really shows what genuine resiliency is. While it is true that most people will never have to endure a life altering event like Ray did, most of us will be forced to face difficult times, perhaps even tragic events, during the course of our lives. Human nature often steers us toward despair and heartache. It takes great strength of personal character to rise up in spite of the negative events that life sends our way. The benefits of personal resiliency transcend any singular organization or people group, and they certainly extend beyond the military experience. Ray Mackey is alive to teach us all that there is nothing life can "dish out" that we cannot endure and rise above—even if we are forced to move in a new direction. There is also a lesson that Ray's experience has to teach us beyond the personal; leaders in business and in government will never be challenged more than when they are forced to guide their organizations through periods of great change in response to forces or events that are well beyond their control. Ray was a hardy, resilient soul long before his injury, and that played a significant role in his ability to endure, cope and rise above his circumstances. Leaders in all organizations can follow Ray's example and work to build resiliency into their teams. When difficulty arrives, and it will, leaders of resilient teams composed of resilient people will be better able to bend and snap back. Moreover, leaders need to be personally resilient because they will face "trials of many kinds," while at the helm. The stress of leading a business enterprise can be overwhelming at times, and resilient leaders are better able to rebound when they endure a significant setback. *Take Ray Mackey's example and deliberately develop team resiliency now.*

Chapter Twenty-seven: Coaching is Leadership

I had the great pleasure of spending a year in London as a colonel attending the Royal College of Defence Studies. It was a tremendous experience, personally and professionally. My family and I look back on our time in London with the fondest memories. One afternoon, my Faculty Advisor, Major General Tim Chicken of the Royal Marines, pulled me aside with a cheery air. "Congratulations Lance!" I asked him the basis of his congratulations. "Why, on command. Haven't you heard?" "No Sir, I have not." "Well then, after the seminar, come up to my office and I'll share the note that was shared with me." Sure enough, Major General Angie Salinas, the Director of Manpower at Quantico, Virginia, sent a note to Lieutenant General Sir David Bill, Commandant of the Royal College of Defence Studies, informing him of my selection for command of the 12th Marine Artillery Regiment. I was quite happy with this development, and I quickly shared the news with the only other American at the College, Colonel John Petkosek, U.S. Army. I then walked the two miles to my flat. As I arrived and realized that my wife, Rhonda was not home, and that she might find out the news from John Petkocek's wife, Patti, I thought I had better call Rhonda—immediately. Once I had her on the

136

phone, I asked her if she was sitting down. "Well, I'm sitting on a bus." I told her, "I know where we are going next—Okinawa, Japan. I am going to be the Commander of the 12th Marine Regiment there!" We had never been actually stationed in Okinawa, though I had been there years ago on a unit deployment. I was anxious to hear her reaction. She was immediately positive, seeing it as a new adventure, and so it was!

Commanding an artillery regiment is quite different than command at the battalion level. Now I really was, "the Old Man." I remember walking the halls of the regimental headquarters as a lieutenant and seeing pictures of all the previous regimental commanders and noting how old they looked. Now they did not look so old anymore! I was closer in age and life experiences to the Division Commander than I was to my "young" battalion commanders.

I believed that one of my responsibilities as a regimental commander was to "shield" my battalion commanders from some of the administrative and legal requirements that so often consume a commander's attention by handling the matters that I could at my level. The Marine Corps made this choice easy in one area with the decision to send all sexual assault cases to the colonel level. Now, a battalion commander had to pass these cases up to the Regimental Commander. In a sense, this was a good thing, because those cases tended to be very time consuming and legally complicated.

Battalion command is the first level of command that a leader has a staff and can be independently missioned. For that reason, it is often referred to as the first level of command. As a regimental commander, I had battalions within my organization that I was responsible for effectively commanding and controlling. I think that tactical command and control is probably the part of regimental command that is most obvious, and certainly the one for which the Marine Corps best prepares its senior officers. However, there is another function that I saw as an equally important duty. I believed that coaching my battalion commanders was one of my principal responsibilities, even more important than the time I spent with my own regimental staff.

When I speak of coaching commanders, I am referring to active listening and mentoring, of stepping outside the role of command and control for a moment, and providing counsel, general or specific, from whatever wisdom I had to offer. Coaching requires time and attention, something that is difficult to dedicate during the course of our busy schedules, especially in artillery units in the operating forces. Coaching also requires fostering a trusting relationship with the person being coached; a relationship in which the person receiving the coaching has confidence that the things he or she discusses will not be seen as a weakness in their leadership or performance. The onus on forming this kind of a relationship is on the coach. The coach must deliberately foster an environment in which the person he or she is coaching feels comfortable revealing who they are, their strengths and weaknesses, and their motivations. To arrive at that level of comfort, I found that I needed to be transparent with the person I was coaching by revealing some of what I learned in my own experience, often by the mistakes that I made. Of course, to be that transparent, I had to be comfortable sharing my own weaknesses alongside my strengths.

When I was a battalion commander, I rarely sought out my regimental commander for coaching; and for that I was short-sighted. I know that he would have invested the time and energy with me had I shown more receptivity and desire for his input. The reality is that battalion commanders, no matter how good they are, need coaching. The regimental commander is really one of the few people who can effectively coach a battalion commander. Unfortunately, I did not arrive at this realization until about the point that I was surrendering command of my battalion. I now regard it as a sign of maturity as a leader that he or she seeks out coaching and is receptive to receiving coaching.

I think the fact that I came so late to the realization that I needed coaching as a battalion commander, and thereby missed an important opportunity, helped solidify in my mind the strong desire and commitment I had as a senior commander to prioritize coaching. I knew for me to be an effective coach, I had to be intentional in my approach by showing early in my tenure of command how important it was to me. Despite the busy schedule I kept, I would always "make time" whenever a battalion commander called or came by my office to speak privately. Coaching takes time, which is the most valuable thing I could give my commanders—my time. My battalion commanders quickly learned that they could schedule time with me and ask for my advice or coaching. At that point, they were not asking for mission-oriented direction, but rather, they were seeking out my counsel. Some might call this a teachable moment, but coaching is a bit more nuanced than teaching is traditionally seen to be. Coaching in this sense was more about listening to their issue or problem in a non-judgmental manner, perhaps sharing a similar experience that I had encountered and the lesson I learned from it and offering ideas on how the issue might be approached. When a battalion commander came to me for coaching, he did not need me to solve his problem. Often, he simply wanted a "sounding board" or someone to give him some perspective on the problem, enough that he could form his own decisions, or validate the direction he had already chosen. For me, coaching was about investing in my battalion commanders to help them succeed. That made sense for the effectiveness of the regiment as a whole, but also for the health of the artillery community, because these battalion commanders represented the future of the organization.

Lesson Learned

Coaching is "playing the long game," because you are investing your precious time in people, often in a way that will not have immediate benefit to the organization's mission. The fact that it usually does not have direct, short-term "bottom line" implications is probably a good reason that coaching is often overlooked or insufficiently prioritized by leaders at all levels in most organizations. For me, the importance of coaching came retrospectively as I sensed that I missed a chance to grow more while I was in command at the battalion level. For this reason, I prioritize it as a leader, and I strongly encourage others to do likewise. *Make coaching one of your personal leadership competencies.*

Chapter Twenty-eight: Good Leaders Make the Difference

As a captain I served at Marine Corps Recruit Depot, Parris Island, South Carolina. At one point in my tour there, I was assigned as the 3rd Recruit Training Battalion Logistics Officer, and in that capacity, I was also the Officer-in-Charge of the Battalion Mess Hall. Ours was one of several dining facilities aboard the base, and it therefore presented an easy comparison for management effectiveness, because the facilities, staff, and budgets of all the mess halls were quite similar. Therefore, the most significant variable was the leadership team that managed the respective facilities. The mess halls are all under close scrutiny because of the role they play in recruit training. Schedules are extremely tight and nutritional requirements are carefully monitored. Mess halls have to be ready to feed good, nutritious meals exactly on time for hundreds of recruits. I learned that this was no easy process. Without careful management, a mess line would run out of a main entrée half-way through a training company. Cost-to-feed was based on the number of people serviced at the mess hall, and it was all too easy to be "in the red," meaning that the manager was spending more than he was budgeted to feed his recruits. The trick was to feed high quality meals, on time, at or under the budgeted cost-to-feed.

We had a new Mess Hall Manager, Master Sergeant Yousidis. He did not seem very impressive when I first met him. He was of average height with a slight build. He was generally soft-spoken. Nothing in his outward appearance or demeanor seemed all that impressive. However, as I was soon to learn, Master Sergeant Yousidis was a magician as a Mess Hall manager. Our mess hall was average, which meant that it struggled with its requirements, and vacillated between being on budget and over budget. However, starting not long after he took over responsibility for the mess hall, Master Sergeant Yousidis transformed our mess hall into the best mess hall at Parris Island. Even the dining facility inspectors were awed by how efficiently he managed the mess hall. In fact, he won the Mess Hall of the Quarter Award for eight straight quarters, until he was promoted to Master Gunnery Sergeant and transferred to another assignment. I saw first-hand how one key leader, properly placed, could make a huge impact on his or her organization.

When I assumed command of the 12th Marine Artillery Regiment in Okinawa, Japan, that included ownership of the regimental mess hall aboard our small base at Camp Hansen where the regimental headquarters resided. Once again, as I had experienced almost a quarter century before, I had a mess hall that in recent history had not distinguished itself in a positive way. However, just like last time, we had a new Mess Hall Manager, Master Sergeant Steele, who came in and quickly made a big difference. In fact, he told us at the outset, "I plan to win a lot of awards with this mess hall." I think our expectations were not nearly so ambitious, given the relatively humble state that the mess hall was in when he took over. However, he was very confident that he could transform our mediocre mess hall, one of only two mess halls on Camp Hansen, into an award winner. Master Sergeant Steele started immediately to put his transformation plans into effect, and the change was obvious within a matter of weeks. You could tell it as soon as you walked into the mess hall. Now it was squeaky clean, even during the messy mealtime rush. All the lines were running smoothly, and regardless of when you went in, they did not run out of food items. The salad bar was well stocked with fresh salad, and the beverage station was clean and well supplied. Morale was up among the mess hall personnel, which included both Marines and Japanese civilians. The food was good, and patrons were enjoying the service. Soon, people who had been accustomed to eating at the other mess hall at Camp Hansen started eating at our 12h Marines Mess Hall.

They heard it had a new manager and that the food was good. They wanted to see what "all the buzz was about."

Master Sergeant Steele did not win Mess Hall of the Quarter the first time. He apologized for that, but there had been a lot of corrections to make in the way the facility was managed, and he had to get everyone on board for his plan to break away from the mediocre and start winning. He started winning, and he won Mess Hall of the Quarter every quarter after that, until he was transferred a couple years later. Our mess hall became a source of unit pride. We would host meetings and functions there, because it provided us an opportunity to showcase our professionalism. Master Sergeant Steele was not satisfied with reaching a state of success just to win awards. He continued to innovate, looking for ways to improve the dining experience for all our patrons, while keeping within our budgetary constraints. When he left, he had improved the mess hall to the point that it was the best mess hall on Okinawa, and one of the top mess halls throughout the Pacific.

So how did Master Sergeants Yousidis and Steele turn their mess halls around so effectively? For one thing, they were both was completely competent and knowledgeable. Both leaders knew well how a mess hall should be operated because they had experienced that before in other locations. Both leaders knew the individual jobs and responsibilities of the whole team, and they were able to teach and coach the young Marines so that they better understood "what right looked like." They had high expectations for their entire teams, and they held people accountable, but they did that in a positive way. Even when these two leaders were not physically present, you could see their influence there, as every person knew their job and worked hard to be the best they could be. The winning attitude that these leaders inspired was infectious. Finally, both leaders invested a tremendous amount of personal energy, especially at the outset, to bring about the transformation. Inspiring and leading change requires much the same personal energy investment as entrepreneurship does. Master Sergeants Yousidis and Steele did not have any new resources available to make them successful. They were, however, good stewards of the resources that they already had at their disposal.

Lesson Learned

The two mess hall success stories offer a program evaluation opportunity, because in both cases, all variables were held constant, except the leadership of the organization. They did not have more money, a different staff, a new facility, or new patrons. Everything of significance was the same as before the variable of their leadership was introduced. From this we can conclude from a program evaluation standpoint, that the leader's intervention was the causal factor in the success of the mess halls in both cases. I believe that leaders make the difference. When factors of organizational success are compared, the single most important element is usually the presence of key leaders properly positioned within the organization or team. While there are many reasons why even good organizations fail, the one common factor that I have seen in success is the contributions of individual leaders. In his book, "Good to Great," Jim Collins makes a very similar point when he observes that great companies started by getting "...the right people on the bus (and the wrong people off the bus)...," even before the company determined its corporate strategy. That was Collins' way of describing the critical importance of finding the best people for the position—and as necessary, removing those who are not right for the position. *Look for your Master Sergeant Steeles and find ways to posture them so that they can "win lots of awards."*

Chapter Twenty-nine: Making Pancakes

The Subtle Art of Showing You Care

One of the unusual things about commanding a unit over in Okinawa was that a majority of my people were far away from their families. That realization seems to really "hit home" during traditional family holidays like Thanksgiving and Christmas. Many service organizations such as the Red Cross and the USO are sensitive to this and try to offer some support, some "taste of home." Likewise, commands are attuned to the challenges associated with holidays spent separated from family, and many try to host events like unit Christmas parties to foster morale.

As a regimental commander, one of the traditions I tried to start was Breakfast in the Barracks on Christmas Eve. This event involved serving breakfast to all the Marines and Sailors of Headquarters Battery, 12th Marines in their barracks. The idea was to select one of the lounges and re-purpose it temporarily as a place to serve up a large, hot meal. The event required no small amount of planning, and a lot of help from volunteers! My own personal contribution was made-to-order pancakes. My grandfather used to make buttermilk pancakes for our family when we went to visit him, something I remember with fondness. I thought that I could take that idea to a grander scale and serve my Grandfather's pancakes to all the Marines. A day or two before the event, I made a very large batch of pancake batter using the old recipe (multiplied many times over) and refrigerated it until the morning of the event. On Breakfast in the Barracks morning, we swooped into the re-purposed lounge, and set up a pancake factory! As Marines would file through, I made them pancakes. Of course, that was only one of the entrees we provided, but it seemed to "set the tone" for what I wanted to achieve. From what I could tell, the event was a real success.

Lesson Learned

Organizations like to talk about how much they care about their people. In fact, it is becoming increasingly popular to extol the positive corporate culture that a given organization seeks to foster. My sense is that there is goodness in creating a work environment in which people enjoy serving. However, to be effective, organizations have to get beyond "mere lip service," and actually demonstrate with their actions that leaders genuinely care for the people with who they serve. Although my Breakfast in the Barracks event may be an extreme example of the idea, and will not be right for every organization, the principle is universally applicable. Look for tangible ways to convey that yours is an organization that genuinely values its people. No one can express this more clearly than the leaders themselves through their own personal involvement. *I suggest you find your own way to "Roll up your sleeves and make Grandpa's pancakes."*

Chapter Thirty: Making the Tough Call

I learned at an early point in my career that leaders are sometimes called upon to make difficult decisions regarding the people with whom they serve. I found that the people decisions, particularly when they involved taking actions which would adversely affect an individual's career potential, were usually more difficult than managing equipment, schedules, and budgets. I think this is natural, and probably a good thing because it can give a leader motivation for greater circumspection and deliberation before he or she makes a decision that could end or substantially limit the career prospects of a member of the team. However, making those tough calls is part of being an effective leader and is often necessary for the benefit of the rest of the team. Ultimately, leaders bear an organizational responsibility to make the tough calls.

Artillery is a dangerous business. It is dangerous in both peacetime and in war. Artillerymen are thoroughly drilled in the very specific procedures of properly firing a howitzer. Members of the gun crew can be seriously injured or killed if they fail to follow procedures. Meticulous attention to detail is absolutely demanded, and no short-cuts or deviations are ever tolerated. Safety is inherent in the process, so adherence to proper procedure is an absolute requirement. I once had a regimental commander who made it his policy to relieve a howitzer section chief if he ever caught a Marine on a gun without hearing protection during live fire missions.

I still remember an episode when I was a lieutenant in which a failure to follow proper procedures almost led to tragic results. We were training at Marine Corps Air Ground Combat Center, Twentynine Palms, California, and were conducting live fire missions. One of the fire missions called for the use of a mechanical time fuze, which is a fuze set on the gun line to cause the round to explode at a certain point in the terminal trajectory based on elapsed time—preferably on top of the enemy. Very shortly after our guns fired the first volley, there was a mid-air explosion in front of the gun line. We believe the gun crew incorrectly set the fuze for 1.5 seconds rather than 15 seconds. The result of this premature explosion was shrapnel going everywhere, including back toward the battery! A large chunk of hot shrapnel impacted against the side door of one of our gun trucks that was driving behind the gun line, leaving a large dent in the steel door on the driver's side, about four inches below where the driver rested his left arm. We could have easily had an arm amputation if it struck just a little higher. Fortunately, no one was injured. I learned an important lesson that day. I would never tolerate any relaxation in discipline or procedures when it came to training. The business end of the artillery trajectory is also fraught with risk. In war, there have been too many cases of artillery mistakenly firing on their own troops. Even in the fog and friction of combat, that is inexcusable.

The enforcement of standards of operation and procedure is a basic responsibility for artillery leaders. I expected all my subordinate commanders to join me in enforcing the standards. Unfortunately, we experienced a couple firing incidents. One of the incidents resulted when one of the guns was pointed in an entirely different direction than the other guns in the battery during daytime firing, and no one noticed until the battery fired a round that missed the impact area. In fact, it almost flew off the military installation altogether. The fact that this happened in mainland Japan where the presence of American military is not very popular with the local Japanese citizenry, only served to complicate this unfortunate and altogether preventable incident. Every artillery firing incident requires an investigation. Afterwards, the Battalion Commander makes an assessment of the actions he deems necessary, to include holding those leaders involved responsible, and taking disciplinary actions against them if necessary. In this case, the Battalion Commander decided to hold off in relieving the culpable Battery Commander, and to counsel him instead, and to warn him of the consequences of any further leadership failures.

Unfortunately, this story does not end well, because a few months later, the same battery had another live-fire incident, this time involving small arms. The Battalion Commander and I spoke at length on this issue, and given the circumstances, I supported his decision to relieve the Battery Commander for cause. Sometimes a popular officer is simply not obtaining satisfactory results, often as a result of a lack of support from his team of subordinate leaders. My sense is that was the case in this circumstance. Ultimately, the commander is held responsible, but for these procedural failures to occur, several other leaders also failed to do their job, and in this sense, they let their unit and their commander down.

Lesson Learned

Making a tough call, such as firing a valued employee, is never easy, but in my mind, it is sometimes justified if that person is endangering others by their behavior, or if their work is of such a substandard nature that it is reflecting poorly on the organization as a whole.

Leaders should be loyal to their people, but that loyalty has to be carefully balanced with their loyalty to the team, and to the organization itself. Good leaders have the fortitude to act decisively when they must, and the wisdom to discern when this decisive action is required. *Be ready to make the tough call.*

Chapter Thirty-one: Be Bold and Innovate

As a regimental commander, one of the initiatives that I sought to put in place was the 12th Marines Mentorship Program. The concept was simple enough. I asked that every Marine and Sailor in the regiment find a mentor with whom to work. The program was completely voluntary, both on the part of the mentor and of the person being mentored. The program was not tracked, nor did anyone report on the results. I assembled groups in the regiment and presented them with a brief in which I defined mentorship, explained the role of the mentor and the role of the person seeking mentorship; then I challenged the young Marines to seek out a mentor. Likewise, I challenged older Marines within the regiment to be ready to agree to provide mentorship, if they were asked.

I knew from personal experience the importance of good mentorship at key moments in a person's career, and I wanted to sponsor a unit-wide push to make mentorship a more natural phenomenon within my organization. I saw the inherent goodness in mentorship, and it was more important to me to create the conditions for it to occur more naturally than it was to construct it in a manner that I could actively manage it. That was the point. All the best mentorship that I have been afforded by others, or that I have provided others, came very naturally as a fruit of a relationship. My purpose was to help others see how easy mentorship could be and to make it more common—starting with my organization. I do not know how well my plan worked, since I did not track it. I was reminded of my mentoring program years later by one of my senior officers who confided that he was still in touch with and providing mentorship to a couple younger officers; and he started that based on our mentorship program.

My intention in relating this story is not so much to champion mentorship, but to point out that leaders will find it all too easy to focus internally on just making their organization operate as it should. Doing something more, such as sponsoring a new initiative, requires a great deal of personal energy, and the rewards for a successful initiative may be deferred for quite some time. In fact, many good initiatives will simply not work, not because they were not worthwhile, but because other demands and requirements took priority. Moreover, not everyone in an organization will share the leader's enthusiasm for a bold, new initiative, especially when many feel like they are already struggling just to perform their current duties in the same way they have been doing them. Change is tough, and it requires a great deal of energy to break homeostasis; in fact, I believe that leaders who push for bold changes require much the same enthusiasm and personal energy as do entrepreneurs.

Lesson Learned

My belief is that good leaders cannot help it. They feel compelled to innovate, to try new things, and test new ideas. They know that they will often strike out, but they continue to return to the plate for another chance to hit one over the proverbial fence. Good leaders want passionately to make their organizations better, and they are less concerned with who gets the credit. Good leaders want their people to succeed, not only in the present, but throughout their careers, and so they invest in people, especially young leaders who show potential. Good leaders have an internal drive, a feeling of never being satisfied that they have done enough, and so they continue to innovate, even when their organization is succeeding in the current sense. Good leaders do not allow themselves to fall into the complacency of "good enough," believing that they must continue to improve their organizations. My Grandfather used to tell me when we were out quail hunting, "You can't get a bird if you don't shoot." His simple point was that, though there is a cost for action; that is the only way to seize an opportunity. *Be bold and innovate.*

Chapter Thirty-two: The Sergeant Major's Couch

Having Others Who Reinforce Your Message

When I was the Commander of the 12th Marine Regiment in Okinawa, Japan, I benefitted from having a strong staff and a great command team. I knew from my experience as a battalion commander that I simply could not be everywhere that I deemed important, and I needed others who could trumpet my message in areas I was not present. Both my executive officer and my sergeant major proved to be exceptionally effective leaders, and I relied on them to help me in all areas of command. I made a point when I took command of a unit to provide my sergeant major with a list of guidance points, something to begin a discussion between us and help me to communicate my basic expectations of this most critical position. I believed that establishing a strong relationship with my sergeant major should be one of my earliest priorities.

The military goes to great trouble to select the most fully qualified officers for command and goes to no less effort in selecting the top senior enlisted advisors to the commanders. More than any other person, the unit sergeant major is the one closest to the Commander; the one best postured to learn how the boss thinks and what his or her real intent is with any initiative, plan or program. Commanders often confide in their sergeants major, sharing the full story and background that led to their opinion or set of priorities. For that reason, the sergeant major often has background insight into the real intent that the commander has for his or her agenda and is sometimes able to project forward and anticipate how the commander would react to a new development.

No commander thinks that he or she is difficult for their people to understand, but how many bosses in any kind of organization, spend much time seeking to determine what their people are really thinking and whether their message is really resonating with the team? Even if the boss sincerely wanted unvarnished feedback, how would he or she go about obtaining it? As a regimental commander, I wrestled with these questions myself. With my staff, I could simply seek them out and pull them aside to discuss my ideas, and quickly ascertain whether they genuinely understood and agreed with my ideas and plans. However, obtaining that level of one-on-one interaction and feedback was significantly more challenging beyond my staff and subordinate commanders. Fortunately, I had a "secret weapon" at my disposal, someone who "spoke McDaniel," and could transcend all organizational levels to extract ground truth from the people who were actually executing the plans. My "secret weapon" was my superb Regimental Sergeant Major, Sergeant Major William "Bill" Grigsby, who was particularly effective at helping me spread my message and in providing me the highest quality feedback on what people were really thinking. Sergeant Major Grigsby was also gifted at conveying my priorities to all levels of the organization in terms that were meaningful to them.

I learned a lesson as a battalion commander that one way to determine whether your sergeant major is organizationally effective was to watch and see who sought them out. Of course, the Sergeant Major would speak with people as he walked about the work-spaces and living areas, but a truly effective sergeant major would have leaders of all ranks coming by to see them —deliberately seeking his or her counsel. That meant that people respected the Sergeant Major's opinions and judgment, and it also meant that they trusted the Sergeant Major. That is exactly what I saw from the beginning with Sergeant Major Grigsby. Everyone from junior non-commissioned officers to seasoned field-grade officers and senior enlisted people would ask to speak with Sergeant Major Grigsby. The Sergeant Major's couch in his office seemed a comfortable place to ask questions and gain insight from a man who saw the organization from both the macro and micro levels. Sergeant Major Grigsby had a gift for being approachable and real genius for conveying complex ideas in layman's terms.

Lesson Learned

I think good leaders continue to learn throughout their careers, and I admit that I learned a great deal from serving with some of the finest senior enlisted leaders in the Marine Corps. Sergeant Major Grigsby showed me the real importance and value of having a trusted agent who could really "keep his hand on the pulse" of the organization, and could walk my message down to the lowest level, and make it relevant to everyone along the way. This may seem like a lesson for military leaders, but what can business leaders derive from this? Strategic communications are often geared as much for organic consumption across and within a large business enterprise as they are for external audiences. Organizations need people like Sergeant Major Grigsby who can assist the senior executive in promulgating his or her message in meaningful and relevant terms, and who are genuinely accessible by people throughout the organization, and thereby provide a feedback loop for senior-most executive leaders. Sergeant Major Grigsby was an extraordinary example, but the basic lesson can be applied by any organization. *Find and cultivate people whose talents will assist you in communicating your key themes and messages.*

Chapter Thirty-three: Keep Your Cool

At some point in a leader's career, they will face a circumstance in which someone on their team, intentionally or unintentionally, will undermine some direction they as a leader have given. If you find out about this, it can be infuriating. However, my recommendation is to take a deep breath, and exercise some patience. I have found that people will judge you by your actions, including how well you control your temper. Your team will tend to have confidence in you when they see you demonstrate your competence and your self-control. A singular incident in which someone effectively undermined or countermanded direction or guidance that you provided may not be reason to immediately react and confront the individual.

In one of my assignments, I was the senior officer responsible for the orchestration of all my team's work output. In one instance, I provided very specific instructions on how I desired for a situation to be handled. I gave this direction after our team had experienced the embarrassment of not having the appropriate information available when senior leaders required it during a high-stress period. Soon after I gave the instructions, I overheard one of our team telling his fellow teammates that they should not handle the situation in the manner I had prescribed. He made his argument, though not to me. The result was that the task was not uniformly handled across the team. My initial reaction was to confront the offender, but my honest sense was that he did not intend to countermand my directions. I just think he thought he had a better approach. Rather than reacting in anger, I chose to wait and see how this situation would play out. I much preferred that people follow my lead out of respect for who I was as a leader, and less for my positional authority. In the end, we had an opportunity later to edit the information and align it with what I had initially directed. The individual who seemingly countermanded my direction in time became one of my most trusted team members. He just needed some time to get to know me.

Lesson Learned

I think the more experienced I became as a leader, the less threatened I felt by others who failed to automatically show deference to my authority. I was comfortable with myself, and had the self-confidence to exercise patience with others, even those who did not immediately respond in the way I expected. I reasoned that people would usually respond to my leadership; for some it simply required a little more time and attention to convince them that I was a leader to whom they should provide their whole-hearted support. Rarely is it a good idea to react in anger in the heat of the moment, particularly if you are not sure that the supposed offender really intended to undermine your authority. There may be a time to react in righteous anger, but those times are rare indeed—and you may undermine your own credibility. Take a breath, get the facts, and *keep your cool*.

Chapter Thirty-four: A Time for Executive Intervention

One of the things that a good staff officer learns is that his or her principal role is to support their boss, the executive. This is true at every level in every organization. I always felt that if I was doing my job well, I was anticipating requirements and issues on behalf of my boss. However, once in a while, I confronted a challenge that only the executive could properly handle.

My final active duty assignment was as an Assistant Deputy Director in the Strategic Plans and Policy Directorate on the Joint Staff at the Pentagon. Our boss, the Director of Strategic Plans and Policy, Lieutenant General Frank McKenzie, had invited his Turkish counterpart, Lieutenant General Turkgenci, to the Pentagon for a meeting. Lieutenant General Turkgenci was in Washington for a couple days of meetings. His first day, he was scheduled to meet with a senior official with the Office of the Secretary of Defense (OSD) there at the Pentagon. His meeting with Lieutenant General McKenzie was scheduled for the second day. At the appointed time on day one, Lieutenant General Turkgenci's entourage arrived at the VIP access gate at the Pentagon. Unfortunately, the

OSD officials had not made all the arrangements for an exception to security screening policy, and therefore, Lieutenant General Turkgenci was subjected to the "typical" security screening for people entering the Pentagon. When the Pentagon police asked him to remove his jacket so that they could wand him, he became incensed and strongly objected to the treatment. Ultimately, he turned around and stormed out of the entry point, returned to his motorcade, and departed the Pentagon reservation.

I learned of the incident from the U.S. Defence Attaché to Turkey, an Air Force Brigadier General who had accompanied Lieutenant General Turkgenci on his trip to Washington from Ankara, Turkey. The Defense Attaché called us to tell us of the incident, and to let us know that the whole trip was now in jeopardy. Lieutenant General Turkgenci was so enraged over his mistreatment that he was now refusing to return at all that day for meetings. In fact, he intended to forgo his meeting with Lieutenant General McKenzie, our boss, the following day, and simply return to Turkey. The Defense Attaché felt that there would be repercussions in the U.S. military's relationship with the Turkish military for a while after this diplomatic insult.

After I hung up with the Defense Attaché, I

reconfirmed that our arrangements to bring Lieutenant General Turkgenci into the Pentagon without a security screening were solid. (We had submitted a request days before for a waiver to the policy that would allow us to bring our VIP guest through the VIP entrance without being subjected to any additional screening.) I did not want a repeat of the day one fiasco. Then I called the Defense Attaché back on his cell phone. He was in a gloomy mood. I said, "Sir, please give me Lieutenant General Turkgenci's personal cell phone number." The Defense Attaché gave me the phone number. As soon as I hung up with him, I quickly walked down to Lieutenant General McKenzie's office. He was out, but due back shortly. I explained the whole affair to the Executive Assistant. I did not have to wait long before Lieutenant General McKenzie returned to his office. The Executive Assistant briefly explained the matter to the boss, and I filled in some additional details. Then the boss asked me, "So Lance, what should we do?" I replied, "Sir, I have re-confirmed that we are "good to go" to bring Lieutenant General Turkgenci in tomorrow through the VIP access point--if he will agree to come. I have Lieutenant General Turkgenci's personal cell number. I believe if you call him now, you can persuade him to come." The boss told the Executive Assistant to dial the number.

I could tell that Lieutenant General McKenzie was taking those few moments to decide how he would handle the conversation. Much to my delight, Lieutenant General Turkgenci answered directly, and our boss began as masterful an act of diplomacy as I have ever witnessed. He told Lieutenant General Turkgenci that he had just learned of the incident and he was personally appalled! He apologized profusely and genuinely for the way Lieutenant General Turkgenci was treated. Then he shifted the conversation and made a personal entreaty for Lieutenant General Turkgenci to return to the Pentagon to meet with him as planned, and the boss assured him that he would receive the treatment befitting a VIP guest. He said, "I will be out front to personally greet you and walk you in." Lieutenant General Turkgenci could not refuse the personal request, so he agreed to come in as scheduled. The next morning, I accompanied my direct boss, Brigadier General John Wood and Lieutenant General McKenzie outside as we awaited the arrival of our VIP guest. Soon his motorcade arrived and Lieutenant General McKenzie escorted Lieutenant General Turkgenci into the Building without incident and took him down to his office for a long, friendly meeting. Afterward, Lieutenant General Turkgenci departed the Pentagon and returned to Ankara, Turkey without meeting with any other Pentagon officials. I think he was still frustrated with the way he was treated the day before, but he and Lieutenant General McKenzie were now on stronger terms relationally than if the incident had never happened. Lieutenant General McKenzie managed to turn a diplomatic row into an opportunity to cement an important relationship with his Turkish counterpart.

Lesson Learned

There are probably several lessons to be learned from this episode, but the one that I want to highlight is that sometimes, the executive must become personally involved at the critical moment in a high stakes circumstance in order to bring about the desired outcome. As an Assistant Deputy Director, I realized that we had a crisis unfolding, and I saw the action that we needed to take, but I could not bring this to fruition myself. This was one of those instances in which only the boss, the executive himself, could take the necessary action. The good news is that we were ready, having performed all the necessary coordination from the standpoint of security access, to seize an opportunity. We just needed Lieutenant General McKenzie's help to "land it." At the time, I had not expected Lieutenant General McKenzie to play his role so brilliantly. The cultural context also worked in our favor. Today the two men are friends, a positive development which has helped our two nation's militaries relate during some tense periods. The point here is that senior executives need to be open and ready to personally intervene when the time is right, and the circumstances warrant it. Likewise, the executive must ensure that his or her people are sensitive to opportunities to use their boss as a precision weapon system to achieve a highly desired effect. *Sometimes executive intervention is required.*

Chapter Thirty-five: Keep Your Executive Informed

As a relatively junior officer I learned the old military proverb, "What do I know, who needs to know it, and have I told them?" Clearly the importance of communication is emphasized with this question, but so is the responsibility for people to take an active and personal role in sharing information. All organizations face the challenge of sharing pertinent information in a timely manner with those who need to know it. Typically, when we think of sharing information, we think of communicating laterally, between agencies or departments within an organization, but sometimes the challenge is sharing down—or up.

When I was a newly promoted colonel, I was assigned to Headquarters Marine Corps at the Pentagon. I was posted as the Director of Readiness Branch within the Plans, Policies and Operations Division. That was my first real exposure to working on a top-level staff, and while I had been successful up to that point in my career, this was a whole new experience. I had a small team of military officers and government civilians, and our job was to track, analyze and report on enterprise readiness based on input from all 410 reporting units. We were busy with this role, and our requirements seemed to grow as we were required to support service budget justification. Unfortunately, my boss did not see our activity. I rarely briefed him, because I did not need his assistance, and he seemed busy enough with other demands on his time. The net result was that he concluded that we were less than fully employed, and he felt he needed to give us some of the workload from other branches that seemed more obviously busy. As I pondered this strange situation, I spoke with our Deputy, a fellow colonel, but one who was appreciably more experienced than I was. He reminded me that I probably needed to spend more time interacting with the boss, not just to seek his assistance, but also to keep him apprised of all our activities, even if we did not require his direct input. Based on his advice, I began making a point of scheduling time to keep the boss "up-to-speed" on our activities, which he seemed to appreciate. Another thing I started doing was sending the boss a Weekly Activities report which summarized the work in which we were engaged. Our report also looked forward at upcoming key events on our calendar. After only a few weeks of this, my boss changed his assessment of our level of work. He even pulled me aside and told me frankly, that he had been unaware of just how busy we were. Now he was impressed!

When I returned to the Pentagon to serve on the Joint Staff several years later, we faced a similar challenge of communication with our senior executives. Several, but by no means all, of the Deputy Directorates (military equivalent to a corporate department or division) provided the Director (military equivalent to a corporate Vice President) with a weekly activities report. My team was one that habitually provided a report. When I transitioned from being a Division Chief to become the Assistant Deputy Director, I carried on that tradition, and we placed no small emphasis on providing a well-written weekly report for the Director to consume. I noted that the Director appreciated these reports because he would provide us feedback, ask questions, and sometimes provide new assignments in reaction to our reports. In time, the Director mandated that all nine of the Deputy Directorates should provide a weekly summary of their activities. Further, he wanted us to share these reports among the Deputy Directorates. We were the smallest team, but we were producing as much or more work output than any other team in support of the Chairman of the Joint Chiefs of Staff (senior-most military officer and equivalent to corporate CEO). In fact, our Director often shared some of our activities with the Chairman. Our weekly reports made our contributions more obvious, and when it came time for us to argue for increased staffing to align with our requirements, we became the number one priority for manpower, and received the support of leadership for this personnel re-prioritization and resultant re-alignment.

Lesson Learned

I learned the criticality of keeping my boss apprised of my team's activities, not only to elicit his support, but also to build his situational awareness over time, so that when I approached him with an issue, he had often seen it developing in my weekly reports, and was better poised to render a decision or provide executive guidance. Keeping my boss informed was one of my principal responsibilities. I learned the art of providing the boss with what he needed to know, without burdening him with too much minutia. I also learned that nearly every executive genuinely appreciates receiving activity reports on a regularly recurring basis, often to the extent that they will schedule precious time to digest these reports if they can anticipate receiving them at a particular day and time. *Make it a priority to keep your boss informed on your team's activities, past and future.*

"The painful struggles we would never choose often offer the greatest opportunity for personal growth, and personal growth is the only path to genuine leadership development." Col Lee Ellis, USAF (ret.)

Lightning Source UK Ltd.
Milton Keynes UK
UKHW020943230720
367029UK00008B/129

9 781714 959327